Unfettered Journey
Appendices

Philosophical Explorations on Time, Ontology, and the Nature of Mind

Gary F. Bengier

Copyright © 2020 by Gary F. Bengier

All rights reserved. No part of this publication may be reproduced, distributed, or transmitted in any form or by any means, including photocopying, recording, or other electronic or mechanical methods, without the prior written permission of the publisher, except in the case of brief quotations embodied in critical reviews and certain other noncommercial uses permitted by copyright law. For permission requests, write to the publisher, addressed "Attention: Permissions Coordinator," at the address below.

Chiliagon Press

1370 Trancas Street #710
Napa, California 94558
www.chiliagonpress.com

Published 2020

Printed in the United States of America

Publisher's Cataloging-in-Publication Data

Names: Bengier, Gary F. (Gary Francis), 1955—, author.
Title: Unfettered journey appendices: philosophical explorations on time, ontology, and the nature of mind / Gary F. Bengier.
Description: Napa, CA: Chiliagon Press, 2020.
Identifiers: LCCN: 2020906059 | ISBN: 978-1-64886-004-1
Subjects: LCSH Ontology. | Consciousness. | Time. | Metaphysics. | Philosophy of mind. | BISAC PHILOSOPHY / Metaphysics. | PHILOSOPHY / Free Will & Determinism. | PHILOSOPHY / Mind & Body
Classification: LCC B105.C477 B46 2020 | DDC 126—dc23

First Edition
10 9 8 7 6 5 4 3 2

Contents

TIME FROM INSIDE AND OUT— A SCIENTIFICALLY CONSISTENT VIEW
1 PHILOSOPHICAL VIEWS ABOUT TIME
2 SCIENTIFIC VIEWS OF TIME AND A CONSISTENT PHILOSOPHY

A METAPHYSICAL ONTOLOGY CONSISTING ONLY OF RELATIONS
1 PROBLEMS IN THE ONTOLOGICAL LANDSCAPE
2 REARRANGING THE ONTOLOGICAL FURNITURE
3 VIEWPOINT ON CERTAIN PUZZLES GIVEN A SIMPLIFIED ONTOLOGY

MENTAL CAUSATION—A RELATIONAL ONTOLOGY
1 SIGNIFICANT PROBLEMS OF MENTAL CAUSATION
2 MIND AS RELATIONSHIP
3 KIM'S MAIN PROBLEMS OF MENTAL CAUSATION ANSWERED

REFERENCES
ENDNOTES

Time from Inside and Out—a Scientifically Consistent View

Because we exist within the universe, our viewpoint constrains how we experience time—as flowing forward. Einstein's special relativity (SR) says that there is a space–time continuum, and that our perception of the flow of time depends on our reference frame. In the space–time continuum, space and time are bound up, and time has a similar existence to the three spatial dimensions of length, width, and depth (x, y, z).[1] The continuum would suggest that if we can take a view from "outside," then time is also of a piece, similar to the other dimensions. If this is true, then the reality of time is nothing like our experience. From a perspective outside, the universe and time more resemble an ancient fossil containing a petrified insect, say a dragonfly frozen in amber.

Philosophical views about time from the past century do not adequately account for SR, and those that try to accommodate modern physics commingle other philosophical arguments in inconsistent ways. The view presented here tries to sort out the philosophical arguments.

Philosophical views from the 20th century have been divided into A-theories and B-theories. I argue for a variant of a B-theory, a tenseless theory of time, which is consistent with SR. The A-theories are tensed theories of time and suggest that either only time up to the present moment exists or that only the present moment exists. These do not conform to general relativity theory (GR), that the relative rates that time flows for different reference frames vary, with those reference frames affected by velocity and proximity to mass. "Proper time" is seen in each reference frame on its own clocks, but within GR there does not exist the notion of uniform time that is assumed for the A-theories.

If we employ a new distinction between outside and inside perspectives, then from "outside" time a B-theory meta-description holds, but "inside" time we admit our experience of causality rules what we interpret as time. This view grants a place for the *past, present,* and *future* tensing that is part of experience.

Philosophies of time interweave with metaphysical claims regarding persistence. I combine my B-theory approach with an *endurantist* philosophy of persistence (defined below). This synthesis conflicts with the popular view that *perdurantism* (defined below) is most consistent with B-theories and that endurantism is most consistent with A-theories. The perdurantist view brings along metaphysical baggage (trying to solve the problem of temporary intrinsics), and that a dimensional analysis highlights confusion in the semantics of perdurantism. One can square an endurantist view of persistence with the leading physical theories, and endurantism fits neatly with a B-theory of time.

1 Philosophical Views About Time

A-Theories and B-Theories

Modern philosophical discussion from the 20th century on the nature of time began with McTaggart, a British idealist who might have come to his ideas about time through mystical experiences (McDaniel, 2010). He poses a distinction between the A-series, a tensed ordering of *past, present,* and *future,* and the B-series, a tenseless ordering of *earlier than, later than,* and *simultaneous with* (McTaggart, 1927). Note that the A-series view is commonly accepted by the average person because tense seems real and we can use the "past tense."

While time structures events in the world, McTaggart (1927) argues that time is unreal. First, he says that the B-series presupposes the A-series. McTaggart claims the properties of *being past, being present,* and *being future* are preconditions for the relations of *being earlier than, being later than,* and *being simultaneous with.* Second, he argues that the existence of the A-series leads to a contradiction,[2] and therefore the A-series is impossible. Since the A-series is a precondition, then the B-series is also impossible; therefore, time is unreal. McTaggart's argument created a vigorous philosophical debate. Most philosophers conclude that McTaggart's argument (i.e., that time is unreal) fails. However, they still use his A-series and B-series distinction to advance new theories. These have clustered into two camps, (a) those supporting the B-series idea as paramount, and (b) those attached to the A-series description of time. Let's explore the main outlines of the respective camps.

B-theorists historically object to McTaggart's first argument, which states that the A-series is a precondition for the B-series. If the A-series is not a precondition, then the B-series stands on its own as the proper, prime temporal framework. B-theorists usually think that existence of such a tenseless ordering is an adequate standalone explanation, without precondition. B-theories fit nicely with modern theories of physics, and Einstein's SR, in particular, because B-theorists assume that time is just another dimension similar to the spatial dimensions. If we imagine space as two dimensions (rather than three, for ease of conceptualization), with time as a third dimension, then the space–time manifold is described by a *block universe,* that is, by this block representing four dimensions that we more easily imagine in our three spatial dimensions. As just another dimension, time has the same ontic reality. B-theorists then are *eternalists,* saying that every temporal event exists eternally. From an ontological perspective, all times are equally real.

Supporters of A-theories believe the tensed description in the A-series best describes time. They attack McTaggart's second argument, saying there is no contradiction. The A-theory arguments focus on the feeling that time is passing, giving the strong intuition that time is tensed. Zimmerman says, "Consider some event that is happening, right now—for example, your reading the words in this very sentence. Too late!" (2008, p. 212). It appeals to such powerful intuitions immediately that it suggests the present moment is favored. This defines the A-theory version known as *presentism*, which claims only the present moment exists; both the past and the future have no existence. There are two common variants. Zimmerman says "An intermediate form of the A-theory accepts the existence of past and present events, things, and times; but denies the reality of the future. This is the 'growing block' view of time . . ." (2008, p. 214). The third variant uses the Moving Spotlight theory from C. D. Broad (Broad, 1923), suggesting there is something special about the present moment, but that future and past events and objects exist. Note that, while the variants all employ a four-dimensionalism, presentism does not.

Faced with our strong intuitions that time is tensed, the new B-theorists acknowledge that tensed language about time cannot be eliminated, that "it is a truism that time passes" (Oaklander, 1994, p. 57). They focus on truth conditions for sentences and try to show that B-theories can provide tenseless truth conditions for tensed sentences. For example, the sentence "It is now 1980" can be translated into "1980 is present" (Oaklander, 1994, p. 62). The debates between A-theorists and B-theorists typically are framed in semantic terms, even as philosophers try to describe the nature of time corresponding with facts about the world and our experience.

Theories of Time that Intertwine Psychological Considerations

Some philosophical theories of time take up the A-theory or B-theory approach but then give a nod to science by incorporating ideas from neuroscience or psychology. An example is found in Callender (2008), who favors a tenseless B-theory. His aim is "explaining why people have the powerful intuition that there is a mind-independent Now and don't believe the same about the spatial Here" (p. 340). Callender cites evidence from neuroscience that explains how brains integrate various sensory stimuli, such as vision and hearing. Given varying delay times for signal propagation in the brain, the argument is that via a multisensory temporal integration window, the brain enforces perceptual synchrony to construct a consistent external world. Borrowing Butterfield's framework of the Present Patches theory (Butterfield, 1984), Callender argues that "the present is not an objective metaphysical global entity, but rather a local mind-dependent constructed one" (2008, p. 350). Callender hopes to provide the beginnings of a theory suggesting that our sense of passing time is all in our heads, merely an illusion. This is an attempt to make sense of views from some physicists that time does not exist. I will later note my objections to this theory but will say here that philosophers must be careful not to misinterpret what physicists mean when they entertain theories about the nonexistence of time.

Endurantism and Perdurantism

To round out this discussion of philosophical theories of time, let's outline the related debate between endurantism and perdurantism. Endurantism and perdurantism are two metaphysical theories of the persistence of objects. When we think of objects persisting through time, we usually think that objects come into existence, exist for some time, and then go out of existence. Concrete particulars have persistence. One is reminded of Samuel Johnson's attempt to disprove Bishop Berkeley's immaterialism by kicking a large stone; we may imagine that the stone persisted somewhere on the ground after his kick. There is an ontological question about the nature of this persistence. Outlining the two views, Lewis (2007) says "Something *perdures* iff [meaning "if and only if"] it persists by having different temporal parts, or stages, at different times, though no one part of it is wholly present at more than one time; whereas it *endures* iff it persists by being wholly present at more than one time" (p. 210). From this distinction, the perdurantist takes concrete particulars to be four-dimensional, incorporating the time dimension into the ontic definition of being. Objects take as their objective reality the form of a "space worm" that also occupies the time dimension. In contrast, the endurantist says that a concrete particular exists wholly present at each time. Lewis intends this distinction to be more than a matter of semantics, in fact a fundamental ontic classification of what is.

Perdurance was introduced to solve the metaphysical problem of *temporary intrinsics*, which is the problem of how to account for changing properties within (i.e., entirely intrinsic to) objects. Lewis (2007) says, "Persisting things change their intrinsic properties. For instance shape: when I sit, I have a bent shape; when I stand, I have a straightened shape. Both shapes are temporary intrinsic properties; I have them only some of the time. How is such change possible?" (p. 211). Perdurantists such as Lewis usually say that concrete particulars have many temporal parts, and that the parts overlap. From the overlap of infinitely many temporal parts, perdurantists try to construct a solution to temporary intrinsics.

B-theories are associated with perdurantism, and A-theories are associated with endurantism. Loux (2006) notes that "The far more natural view is one that couples the eternalism of the B-theory with a perdurantist theory of persistence; and the fact is that almost all B-theorists are perdurantists" (p. 235).

2 Scientific Views of Time and a Consistent Philosophy

During the last century scientists studying relativity, quantum theory, and cosmology have produced masses of supporting experimental evidence. Philosophers such as Reichenbach, a student of Einstein, and more recently philosophers like Callender, have used scientific evidence to support their philosophical arguments about the nature of time. A review of the major lines of the philosophical debate suggests that a minority of the arguments look for support from science. Many philosophers still conduct their arguments following the semantic framework voiced by McTaggart. Regarding the metaphysical nature of time, I argue that semantics is the wrong battlefield. Time should be understood as fundamental to all reality, and science offers foundational insights that should frame the philosophical discussion. To provide balance, I turn to thoughts on time described from a scientific perspective.

Theories of Everything as Related to Theories of Time

To bring scientific context let me briefly sketch the current state of theories of everything (TOEs), the whimsical name used by physicists to describe theories aspiring to a grand unification of all the fundamental forces of nature. Physics has strong evidence for Einstein's special and general theories of relativity, and for quantum mechanics. Physics lacks a theory that unites these theories. The field of quantum gravity tries to unify GR with quantum theory. The current Standard Model of particle physics is missing a quantum account of gravity, and therefore there are no satisfactory TOEs. String theory has been a leading TOE contender for much of the past forty years, yet it still lacks consistency and suffers from an absence of clear, testable hypotheses. Moreover, there are too many versions of string theory to discuss them generally. Newer versions of string theory include M-theory and Brane cosmology, a group of theories motivated by string theory and M-theory, which state that our four-dimensional space–time manifold is like a membrane on a higher-dimensional structure. Other theories have various supporters, such as Loop Quantum Gravity Theory (which was founded by, among others, Carlo Rovelli). As theoretical physicists and mathematicians search for satisfactory theories, conjecture abounds, and these theories fundamentally affect views of time. With the current theories covering a landscape of 10^{500} possible universes, essentially everything is possible.

With this overview, I will focus on SR and GR, because any philosophy of time must be consistent with Einstein's theories.

The Space–time Manifold and Relativity

From Aristotle, St. Augustine, and Newton, historical Western views describe space and time as an absolute container, with time ticking away with perfect periodicity. Duration is independent of any observer's frame of reference. Einstein swept this view away. Rovelli (2008) says about GR, "To put it pictorially: with general relativity we have understood that the Newtonian 'big clock' ticking away the 'true universal time' is not there" (p. 3). Large amounts of empirical evidence support Einstein's SR and GR (more generally), and any modern philosophical theory of time should account for its findings or risk irrelevance.

We may illuminate aspects of Einstein's theory by beginning with a simple, cartoon model of a 4-tuple (an ordered set of four elements), to describe a four-dimensional pseudo-Riemannian space.[3] This four-dimensional space–time can be described mathematically by the notation (x, y, z, t), where t represents the time dimension and x, y, z represent the three spatial dimensions. Note that given any future theory of *n* dimensions, then an *n*-tuple answers just as well, so this simplification does not affect the theory of time. Time is distinguished from the spatial dimensions only in that time is unidirectional, as the so-called "arrow of time."

We can describe several ways the *n*-tuple can be filled in. Let's develop two examples to use through this discussion: the first of a particle existing through time, and the second of a particle decaying into two new particles. Imagine for Example 1 that a particle at (x_1, y_1, z_1, t_1) exists; then assume that the particle still exists at (x_2, y_2, z_2, t_2). For this thought experiment, consider that the particle is a stable, elementary particle such

TIME FROM INSIDE AND OUT—A SCIENTIFICALLY CONSISTENT VIEW

as an electron neutrino, designated by v_e, which is not composed of more elementary particles. As a second example, Example 2, imagine that a tau lepton, designated as τ^-, exists at (x_1, y_1, z_1, t_1). Then at t_2, the tau lepton decays into a tau neutrino (v_τ) and a W boson (W–). We might imagine that at t_2, nothing exists at (x_2, y_2, z_2, t_2); that the tau neutrino (v_τ) exists at (x_2, y_2, z_2, t_2); and that the W boson (W–) exists at (x_2, y_2, z_2, t_2). That is, in Example 2 the decay of the tau lepton results in two new particles proximate in space to the original particle. Since tau leptons have a half-life of approximately 2.9×10^{-13} seconds,[4] the period between t_1 and t_2 is small.

Einstein's GR theory says that velocity and gravity distort time. Matter-energy changes, therefore, change the curvature of space–time itself in a dynamic system. GR says that at high relative velocities (and high relative to the speed of light), time flows at a slower rate for the object moving at the high velocity, as viewed by an observer. From the viewpoint of the speedy object, however, time will flow normally, and time for other objects will appear (to that high-velocity object) to flow at a slower rate. This leads to the "Twin Paradox," a thought experiment in which one twin leaves in a spaceship at high velocity, then returns to find he has aged more slowly than his twin. This is not really a "paradox," but instead an accurate description of how time works. There is an asymmetry between the twins because only one has undergone acceleration, and that asymmetry accounts for the age difference. Despite time dilation, in relativity theory there is no possibility that, for example, you may meet a twin of yourself, because as Reichenbach notes, "We must make the assumption that *there are no closed causal chains*" (p. 139). For two events, E_1 and E_2, where E_1 causes E_2, then there cannot also be a causal relationship back from E_2 to E_1, as this would create a closed causal chain. This concept is also known as a "closed timelike curve."

The second time dilation effect begins with Newton's observation that gravitational force is proportional to mass (of particles). Earth exhibits a gravitational force attracting us to its center, and a star exhibits much greater gravitational force on particles and objects in the space that surrounds it. Per GR, any particle (or object, a collection of particles) that is proximate to a large mass also exhibits time dilation, based on distance. Therefore a clock in a satellite circling Earth runs faster than a clock on Earth's surface.[5] Multiple experiments verify this effect.[6] A clock in a spaceship that falls into a black hole would (from the viewpoint of an outside observer) appear to slow down to zero. The spaceship would take an infinite amount of time to even reach the event horizon of the black hole; from the outside perspective, it would never cross it.

Relativity and Time Dilation as Experienced

Before moving on, I should say something about how SR physics affects the human experience. Per SR, all references to "seeing" the clock, or twin, or any object in another reference frame are purely to aid the thought experiment, because there is no possibility in direct human experience for us to so witness the time-dilated reference frame. Inferential evidence for SR and GR can come as close as the need to adjust clocks on GPS satellites.[7] We adjust our theories to account for evidence associated with faraway objects such as black holes. Except for our measurements of particles and their effects, relativity's time dilation effects do not affect our direct sensory input,[8] nor is there any need to adjust our frames of reference to account for it in sensory experience.

Given that evolution refined our adjustment to sensory experience, our perception of time needs nothing other than Newtonian time. Relative time dilation between ourselves and all objects in direct experience is ridiculously smaller than our sensory detection capacity. Any psychological theories of time that try to incorporate relativity are absurd, and a misunderstanding of the theory of relativity. Our human experience of time is one level of description; the fundamental nature of time is at a different level of description. I will address the fundamental nature of time, and then neutrally try to account for time in both non-sentient and sentient existing entities (particles, rocks, and people).

Relativity and Presentism

The time dilation of GR generates problems for philosophical arguments for presentism. Presentism says there exists only a present moment of time, and that both the past and the future do not exist. However, within the relativistic structure, it is difficult to describe what the "present" consists of. Recall our Example 1 with a particle existing at (x_1, y_1, z_1, t_1). If this particle exists near a black hole, then the time until (x_2, y_2, z_2, t_2) can be long indeed. Each element of space (the 3-tuple) undergoes varying amounts of time, depending on the gravitational effects of nearby particles. For a particular particle accelerating through space, moving from (x_1, y_1, z_1, t_1) to (x_2, y_2, z_2, t_2), time also varies. With SR, Einstein described how our Newtonian idea of simultaneity doesn't work, because different observers can disagree about which events are simultaneous. It is impossible to describe the "slice" of space at a particular instant of time neatly in relativity theory. Presentism is only coherent under a Newtonian description of space–time.

Presentism is the most popular version of A-theory within philosophy. Yet presentism is incoherent given SR. SR favors B-theories because time is another dimension similar to the three dimensions of space. Admittedly, the jury is still out, and there are no proven TOEs that include quantum gravity. If SR is accepted as roughly reflecting reality and is not replaced wholesale by a final TOE (and our scientific evidence supports relativity so far), then some B-theory describes the mathematical structure of time within the universe, and the "block universe" view should be accepted.

The Space–time Manifold and Causality

I'll continue to use the cartoon n-tuple to describe how physicists attribute causality relationships among the elements. In Example 1, there is some causality relationship between the electron neutrino existing at both t_1 and t_2 since it is a stable particle. If forces from other particles acting on the electron neutrino had caused it to move in space, say from (x_1, y_1, z_1, t_1) to (x_2, y_2, z_2, t_2), then this would be consistent with the causality rules that apparently exist as evidenced by empirical observation. In Example 2, the observed causality rules dictate that a tau lepton decays within a certain half-life into a tau neutrino and a W⁻ boson, and the resulting particles will be proximate in space to the original particle. Given a particle description of causality,[9] the *n*-tuple provides a useful cartoon.

The space–time manifold exhibits a unidirectional nature to time. Reichenbach notes that an "essential property of time is its *directionality*" (p. 270). The second law of thermodynamics requires that entropy increases. Light radiates only in the forward direction in time. These are additional reasons that it is wrong to think the unidirectional nature of time is a human, cognitive effect. Causality rules and the resulting unidirectional nature of time are a fundamental, constituent structure of the universe.

FIGURE 1

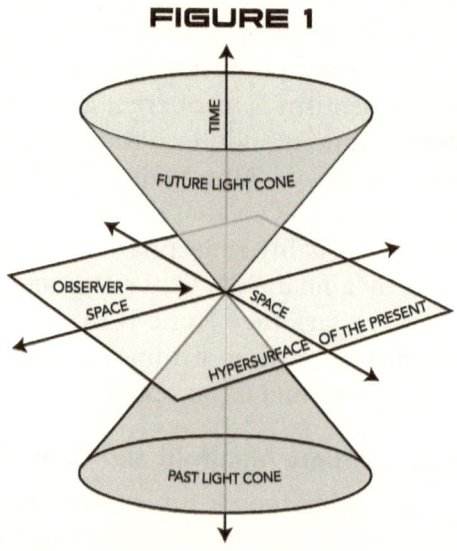

Wikimedia Commons / CC-BY-SA-3.0

Physicists describe the limits on causality relationships by a light cone partition in space–time (Figure 1). To help visualization, the light cone is portrayed with two dimensions representing (the three dimensions of) space and the third dimension representing time. In the diagram,[10] a plane slicing through the cone represents a particular time slice, say t_1. Imagine that a light flash is emitted by an event A (marked by the observer in the diagram). Then as one moves forward in time, the flash spreads out in space (as a circle in two dimensions; and as a sphere in our three-dimensional space) at the speed of light. Successive circles in time spread out like a cone. At any future time, t_2, the circle represents the space containing everything that can be affected by the flash at event A. The cone then partitions space–time into categories of causality.

Every point on the cone in the future forms a light-like pair with event A (i.e., experienced as a flash of light). Every point within the future light cone forms a timelike pair that may be causally affected by event A. Everything outside the light cone in the future cannot be affected by event A (Taylor & Wheeler, pp. 179-183). A past light cone corresponds to the relationships that may be causes of event A. A light ray on the past light cone forms a light-like pair with event A and may be a cause of A. A material particle within the past light cone of event A forms a timelike pair with event A, and may be a cause of event A. Everything outside the past light cone cannot affect event A. Of course, per SR there is no privileged point in space–time, and every point has its own associated light cone, which describes all the possible causes of an event at that space–time point and all the future space–time points that may be affected.

Three added points need to be made about the causality described by relativity theory. First, physicists are Realists about nature and will affirm that such causality rules apply to everything, from particles up through aggregations of particles (including us), and the causality rules work independently of minds. Even if there were no minds, the causality in Example 2 would hold true. Anthropomorphizing particles, the physicist

Potter says that "Most fundamental particles are 'aware' of the elapsed time because they do not 'live' forever; they decay to other fundamental particles with an average lifetime" (p. 3). It is inexact speaking, and misleading to the public (and perhaps to philosophers), to say that by some TOEs "time may not exist." For the particle, even if no minds exist in the universe, the causality rules would hold. In Example 2, the tau lepton would decay within the probabilistic rules of its half-life, and the result would be at some later time that a tau neutrino and a W⁻ boson would appear proximate to the original location of the tau lepton. Whether or not the variables representing time drop out of certain equations in future theories, the causality rules still hold. The rules hold even at the extremes—for example, at the edge of a black hole where time slows to zero. The event horizon of a black hole is "a perfect unidirectional membrane: causal influences can cross it only in one direction" (Finkelstein, pp. 965-967). Our common notions about time, which are fundamentally tied up with causality, always hold. In the sense that is most important to how our existence (and every particle's existence) is organized by causality rules, it is inaccurate to say that "time does not exist."

The second point is that, per SR, causality rules always hold between events that can communicate. The communication speed limit is the speed of light. Despite the difficulty in describing simultaneity under relativity, all correct observers must agree on the time order of two events that could be causally related. The light cone illustrates the causality limits for any particular event and a particular point in space–time. Causality is absolutely preserved. Reichenbach makes this same point when he says that given two events, E_1 and E_2, with E_2 as the effect and E_1 as the cause, then E_2 is called later than E_1, and this is a topological coordinative definition of time order. The events E_1 and E_2 cannot form a closed causal chain, only a closed world line without intersections (pp. 136-141).

The third point is that we do not have a full account of causality. Quantum theory accepts indeterminism. Particles decay based on a probabilistic half-life model. Therefore, at a minimum we can think of the relationship between (x_1, y_1, z_1, t_1) and (x_2, y_2, z_2, t_2), as a rule-based one, with some rules being probabilistic. Per quantum theory, collections of particles can come together at particular points in space–time, and causality rules result in other particles and in the displacement of particles in later time frames. Physicists try to describe the causality rules at the particle level for many particles, but there can be no certainty that this is a correct description of causality.

Endurance, Perdurance, and the Ontology of Objects

I will now return to the metaphysics of persistence—and the alternative views of perdurantism and endurantism—because this metaphysical argument has become interwoven with arguments on the nature of time. I think the perdurantist argument has added to the confusion about time. A metaphysics of persistence in which objects endure (a more common view among scientists) clarifies and supports my claims about the nature of time.

A conventional notion of 'endurance' would include the idea that some particle continues to exist through time.[11] If we assume as in Example 1 that a particle at (x_1, y_1, z_1, t_1) exists, and then assume the particle still exists at (x_2, y_2, z_2, t_2), then the particle endures. We mean by endurance that whatever causality rules are extant continue to allow the particle to be there. If time is distorted (for example because of relativistic time dilation), then presumably some particles will exist for long periods of time relative to an outside observer. For example, if we induced time dilation (by accelerating the particle close to the speed of light in a particle accelerator), then the particle from our perspective would "hang around." This would meet our common definition of "endurance." These examples undercut the perdurantist description of what it means to exist, with their insistence on temporal parts. Causality rules are all that is needed to account for the continued appearance at sequential times of a particular particle. For a particle frozen in time at the event horizon of a black hole, even the causality rules are no longer needed, for causality (and time) has slowed to a stop.

If we wish to account for a particle moving through space, then we want to see the same particle, for example, occurring at (x_1, y_1, z_1, t_1) and then at (x_2, y_2, z_2, t_2).

That is, some causality rules allow the same particle to exist in sequential time periods in proximate locations in space. The same intuition applies to larger collections of particles. Newton's laws of motion, updated for relativity and quantum mechanics, describe the causality rules moving a particle from one place to another in the space–time manifold.

Let's now imagine a macro object composed of a collection of particles. To aid our imagination, we will again invoke a block universe with two spatial dimensions (representing our three actual spatial dimensions), and the third dimension representing time. Then imagine that in our two-dimensional spatial world we wish to talk about a square of particles. At t_1, they fill up the four points (x_1, y_1, z_1, t_1), (x_2, y_2, z_2, t_2), (x_3, y_3, z_3, t_3), and (x_4, y_4, z_4, t_4). Now imagine this square of particles existing through time. We readily imagine that the particles "fill up" a small brick within our larger block of space–time. Now ask us: what is it again that we said exists? We said that a square (of particles) exists. Notice we did not say that a brick exists. Similarly, we say the square persists through time; we do not say the brick persists <u>through time</u>. (The brick describes the trajectory of the square through time.). By analogy, we say that <u>we</u> exist now in time (meaning our collection of particles); we say that our <u>life</u> exists, meaning that we exist through time. Alternatively, we can say that <u>we</u>—ourselves, our bodies, our collections of particles—persist <u>through time</u>.

Our common use of language describes how we experience persisting objects, without the added metaphysical claims of perdurantism. The semantics employed by perdurantists engender confusion, commingling our concepts of our bodies (existing collections of particles at a particular time) and our lives (a description of a collection of particles that evidences existence at a series of points in time, resulting from causality rules). There is no need for "having different temporal parts, or stages, at different times, though no one part of it is wholly present at more than one time" (from Lewis) as a description of an object. The object/event (i.e., particle/causality rules) distinction suffices. To summarize, my reasons for rejecting perdurantism are that it fails to incorporate the variability in temporality evident from SR and that it confuses our understanding of the universe in ways that the object/event distinction can eliminate.

We can make definitive statements about particles, within a description suitable to particles (the lowest level we yet have an ability to talk about with any empirical evidence). Physics can inform the discussion at higher levels of description. Physics can suggest that the strong nuclear force, the electromagnetic force, the weak nuclear force, and the gravitational force account for many interactions that are observable in matter. They account for an object's surface (a primary quality), whose smoothness we can feel (a secondary quality). Physics suggests how the property of a surface may emerge through the interactions of the fundamental forces.

The perdurantist claims are in service to another metaphysical puzzle, solving the "problem" of temporary intrinsics. When we make statements about collections of particles, however, then we enter into semantic distinctions. My example with four particles forming a square is simple enough for us to keep track of, and semantics does not hinder understanding a "square." (I am claiming a fundamental identity only for each particle; the square is a mental construction of particles which may or may not have any further identity in nature.) Semantic identity claims can create paradoxes, such as the Ship of Theseus: Plutarch described the ship preserved by the Athenians, replaced plank by plank as each decayed, and asked whether the ship remained. The problem of temporary intrinsics that perdurantists hope to solve could be a similar problem. The problem comes about by trying to solve a problem at an incorrect level of analysis. If we begin at a particle level of analysis, and then describe causality rules which result in particles at a later time, then we can account for change, the heart of the problem of temporary intrinsics. We need not get lost in the semantic jungle found at higher levels of description.

The "Outside" Versus the "Inside" Distinction

I have identified two relevant sets of notions from a review of the scientific description of time. The first is that, per SR, time is another dimension of a four-dimensional manifold, and while time is unidirectional (an important difference from the three dimensions of space), in other respects it is still a complete dimension. It, therefore, follows that <u>all</u> of the time dimension exists in the same fashion that the dimensions of space exist.[12] The philosophical arguments for the existence of only the "present" slice of time (presentism), or for the existence of parts of the block, fail to be consistent with relativity. The philosophical view most consistent with scientific theory of SR is that the full "block universe" exists, a B-theory view of time. The second set of notions from physics is that the universe functions through strict causality rules. Whatever may come of future theories that might eliminate the time variables from mathematical models of the universe, the causality effects will remain. Therefore, the most important effect of time—in fact, what time might *be*—should exist in all future scientific descriptions.

Descriptions of the universe from the view of physics are mathematical descriptions, supported by empirical observations. Whatever our scientific theories ultimately can say about the fundamental nature of the universe, it is a good guess to think that a mathematical description is fundamental. These mathematical views describe the universe from the outside, essentially from a "God's eye" (Archimedean) viewpoint. The theories carry no requirement that the view from outside describes the view from inside. Moreover, the definition of "view" is not limited to a purely cognitive description. It is unnecessary to say that our view of time "flows," that our particular experience of "the present," is a cognitive illusion. The view from inside is subject to ontological reasons driving our cognitive intuitions. A theory of time can embrace our intuitions about time, yet simultaneously can accept a view (from the "outside") of time as eternal.

I now come to the main thesis. I think this distinction can obviate the semantic war between A-theories and B-theories. The major distinction, right in front of us, is the distinction between <u>outside</u> and <u>inside</u>. Mathematics gives us the capacity to view the universe from outside. Meanwhile, we are all locked inside the universe, in the cycle of causality dictated by fundamental laws of causation, like hamsters on a wheel. No matter the mathematics, we cannot stop turning.

Maybe time itself is an emergent phenomenon,[13] which emerges because of the relations among the basic ontological elements comprising the universe and the causal rules that dictate certain relationships. Maybe some of these relationships create the relationship that we, and every non-sentient particle, interpret as time. Therefore, it is wrong to say that "time does not exist" or that "time is an illusion." Time is surely as real as the emergent property of a surface, which our physics suggests can result from the molecular bonds between particles. We may hold an Archimedean view of time from the outside and simultaneously recognize that, inside the space–time manifold, we are subject to the real rules of causality we interpret as the flow of time.

For much of the past century, philosophers have followed McTaggart onto the semantic battlefield, continuing the argument between A-theories and B-theories of time. Modern science—and philosophy informed by science—can embrace the fundamental premises of both simultaneously. Relativity favors a B-theory view that all of time is eternal; it simultaneously allows for the causality that underlies A-theories of past, present, and future. In his exposition of GR, Reichenbach notes that "We notice that the *intuitive basis* of time order has been retained. The relativistic theory of gravitation does not destroy the intuitive character of time" (p. 272). By embracing the inside/outside distinction and abandoning a narrow semantic approach, philosophy can embrace a more harmonious scientific basis for understanding the nature of time.

Conclusion

Scientific theory supports an approach that preserves intuitions from both the philosophically opposed A-theories and B-theories about time. We can find consistency with SR if we embrace the outside/inside distinction. From an Archimedean perspective, all of time endures; from our viewpoint, inside the physical universe, causality relationships alone would explain our perception[14] of the flow of time. The distinction allows for our perception of past, present, and future, which results from the working of fundamental causality rules we cannot escape. Causality rules "connect the dots" between particles and times in the block universe. Yet consistent with SR, the fourth dimension of time exists as fully as the three dimensions of space and is equally as complete.

Our common notions of endurance suffice to describe how objects persist from one time to another. Contrary to the approach of many philosophers, this view of the nature of time—based around a B-theory meta-view—is most consistent with an endurantist view of the persistence of objects.

The shocking result of this description of time is that from an "outside" perspective, it is "all done," all of a piece. We trace our lives, and our existence, as a worldline in space–time, and that world line occupies only a thin sliver in the block universe description. We are a dragonfly frozen in amber. Yet we experience causality rules that we interpret as time, granting a place for the *past, present,* and *future* tensing that is part of our experience. Whether time exists in the mathematical formulas in any ultimate theory of everything, time will surely continue to exist in our experience of the world.

A Metaphysical Ontology Consisting Only of Relations

My aim is to offer a simplified metaphysical ontology that is logically consistent, and consistent with scientific experimental evidence. The hypothesized ontology offers a different way to view 'relations' in the spirit of Quine's "desert landscapes."[1] I first argue that relations can do the work ascribed to 'properties,' and there is no need for properties. The provisional ontology then is further adjusted to the scientific evidence, step-by-step, to open a path to understanding the world from an upside-down perspective. The result is a radical metaphysical handstand, a different way to view the ontology of physical reality. I offer a hypothesis about *what there is*, to say only two elements need to populate the ontological table, namely, *bolts* and *booms*, and those fall from our current conception of relations. The simplified ontology hypothesis offers ways to untangle several puzzles in the philosophy of mind and in physics.

1 Problems in the Ontological Landscape

Here let me say a few things about the minimal ontological elements traditionally considered to exist, and some problems this formulation poses considering modern scientific understanding.

Minimal Elements Having Existence in Classical Ontologies

A major concern of ontology is with *what there is*, what things there are which have *existence*. Employing the ontological elements that have come down through the Western philosophical tradition, most philosophers and people in the street still talk about objects, properties, and relations. Other elements have been proposed for a complete ontological table, but I will focus on these as more than enough. Scientific evidence suggests that the ways these three elements are used to describe the physical world are not correct.

While philosophers have espoused a wide range of opinions about the ontology of the universe, certain philosophical ideas have seeped into common usage, characterizing the way we describe the world. In common thought, the furniture of the universe begins with some stuff, some substance, of which macroscopic objects are composed. The individual substance has attached to it properties, which in some fashion are "inside" the substance (lacking a better "location" to place properties). We think both the stuff and properties really exist. Between and among objects (made of substance), there are relations: for example, that the planet Neptune is "larger than" Earth, or that Sue sits "between" John and Paul (a triadic relation). We don't commonly think that relations really exist, but invoke a nominalism, thinking of relations as *post res* to the objects which are their *relata*.[2] Substance (or my preferred term, objects), properties, and relations are fundamental ontological furniture.

A 'property,' or something like it, seems to be necessary ontological furniture when talking about the world. Some philosophers hold that to be a property is no more than to confer a 'power' or 'capacity' on its possessor. This concept begins at least with Plato, with the Eleatic stranger suggesting in defining existing things that "I'm saying that a thing really is if it has any capacity at all, either by nature to do something to something else or to have even the smallest thing done to it by even the most trivial thing, even if it only happens once.

I'll take it as a definition that *those which are* amount to nothing other than *capacity*" (pp. 247d-e). One of the main ontological tasks for properties is to account for certain phenomena: they carry causality as this 'capacity,' they provide a *fundamentum in re*[3] to save the phenomena. For example, we say two electrons repel each other because they both possess the property of having a negative charge. Many properties describe deterministic powers, such as Newton's inverse square law for gravitational attraction. Others are non-deterministic powers, such as the spin of an electron. In another role, philosophers of language argue that properties can be truthmakers[4] in a sentence. Such properties are the existing elements that make the proposition true.

Compared to properties, relations have held a second-class status in ontology. As early as Aristotle, monadic properties were thought to inhere in the substance, providing the basis for a relation between the *relata*. From the Scholastics onward, philosophers evolved both realist and nominalist views toward relations, with relations either conceived as real entities, or as stemming from reason and existing only in the mind. Leibniz thought that relations did not correspond to anything in the real world, upholding a nominalism. Frege and Peirce formalized a relational logic a century ago, extending logic rather than ontology. In part due to the classification ambiguity for relations, properties have held a dominant ontological role, and relations were given secondary consideration. I would hazard that another reason for the ambivalence stems from difficulty in characterizing what the relations do—that is, any causative power we typically associate with anything perceived as existent—because of their polyadic nature, which violates intuitions that causation is tied to a location.

Classical Ontology Challenged by Scientific Experimental Evidence

Science is at odds with several of these commonly held ontological views. Experimental evidence raises questions about whether properties have a more primary role than relations, whether properties even exist at all, and whether objects (such as particles in a particular space–time location) exist in the manner we imagine for substantial objects.

In contrast to philosophers, physicists have shown a particular awareness of the importance of relations. For example, the four fundamental forces, more accurately described as "fundamental interactions," are chiefly descriptions of relations among classes of matter.[5] The property of mass is exhibited when some fundamental particles interact with the Higgs field. This formulation suggests something more like a relation at work rather than a property found in any one object (here taken to be a particle). As another example, some partial theories of quantum gravity imagine a lattice structure of points and connective edges (Smolin, 2002, p. 116), corresponding to objects and relations, respectively. To conform to general relativity (GR), the lattice is dynamically changing. The dynamic lattice has been mathematically described as a spin network (Rovelli & Smolin, 1995), and at the Planck scale is the spin foam comprising the smallest discrete definition of space. The edges of the lattice are the active elements, with the points mathematically disappearing from the equations. These are examples of scientific theories relevant to whether properties have priority over relations. The evidence is better interpreted to recommend the reverse.

Two of the most puzzling results in physics are the evidence from the double-slit experiments (of photons and other particles), and the measurements suggesting that Bell's inequalities are violated. I will describe both sets of results in further detail. In summary, the double-slit experiments suggest that light has both a wave nature and a particle nature, with the experimental results dependent upon the measuring method (and, therefore, it seems on the observer). Particles, therefore, are not (only) entities existing in a particular location in space–time. The measured violations of Bell's inequalities suggest that the particles are not local—there does not exist a particular object at a particular place in space–time—and so our concept of things existing in space–time is flawed. Together, this evidence questions whether objects exist at particular points in space–time.

Modern philosophers have raised the same questions. Ladyman et al. question both the secondary status of relations and the existence of individual objects. Regarding the two most important theories in physics of the twentieth century, quantum mechanics (QM) and GR, they summarize a body of evidence to say "QM and GR give us every reason to believe that the Realists must interpret the theories as describing entities whose identity and individuality are secondary to the relational structure in which they are embedded" (Ladyman, Ross, Spurrett, & Collier, 2010, p. 144).

The ontological elements used commonly in conversation clash with scientific evidence. Philosophical ontology should not be antithetical to empirical science. Looking for consistency, I propose to rearrange, and even to eliminate, some of the ontological furniture used to describe the world. The new arrangement conforms to a philosophical scientific realism,[6] but a realism in which the elements are turned on their head.

2 Rearranging the Ontological Furniture

In this section, let me play the universal decorator, rearranging the ontological furniture. I offer an ontology explaining our real universe that consists of fewer elements, with some descriptions of traditional elements rearranged.

A Sparse Ontology

We are embedded in the universe, and that fact profoundly circumscribes the way we perceive that it works. Correspondingly, our conversation is predicated on the way we parse the constituents of the universe, so it is difficult to be easily understood while redefining meanings for our language terms. To avoid these difficulties, I must take a roundabout approach to describe a new ontological framework. I shall begin with a few assumptions and inferences via logic,[7] and propose a starting structure for a sparse ontology. I will hold this framework up to the light of scientific evidence, identify inconsistencies and, as a result, will turn it on its head.

Let us agree that reality consists of all that has existence, whether those things exist in the dimensions we can perceive, or whether those things exist in other unseen dimensions. We perceive four dimensions of space–time, even as the best current scientific theories postulate further dimensions. One aim is to describe the minimal ontology that is logically conceivable and that can account for a physically closed universe.[8] It seems that every table of ontological categories, no matter how sparse, must provisionally admit *objects*, and objects[9] can be said to have existence. The smallest object that we may imagine from our thought experiment is an exemplar of such an admitted object (for a mental picture of the smallest physical object, imagine a particle, or better, a point[10] in a lattice). It provisionally fills out the first category in the ontological table.

The table of ontological categories describes existent things. Existence[11] seems to necessitate its opposite, nonexistence. Therefore, I will accept the negation of existence as a fundamental concept.

Let me employ a cartoon construct to advance the philosophical discussion, holding briefly in abeyance an explanation of how these ideas fit with the results of a scientific experiment. I think at the end of the argument I can make clear that the ontology is consistent with SR, GR, and QM.

We might simplistically[12] conceptualize the physical universe as a spatiotemporal construct, with coordinates in the fabric of space–time at the Planck scale. Then at every point in space–time, either the smallest object exists or it does not.[13] When it is true to say that a particular object exists—in the simplest case, as small as one point in space–time, then that object must have existence as some point(s) in the space–time

A METAPHYSICAL ONTOLOGY CONSISTING ONLY OF RELATIONS

manifold.[14] That is all I shall say about nonexistence versus existence (though I shall assume nonexistence as a complement to existence). Non-Being has been an unresolved ontological problem since Plato, and this portrayal glosses over many issues. Acknowledging these difficulties, I will continue to my main objective rather than try to add more to that philosophical conversation.

Next, we may ask, are there any other necessary categories in our ontological table? If we imagine, say, two or three smallest objects, then we must necessarily imagine there can be a *relation* between the smallest objects. The objects are the *relata* between and among which a relation is said to hold. Logically, therefore, relation enters any descriptive ontology if the existent universe is more than a monism.[15] Yet, to respect the long philosophical debate, it seems unclear whether relations can be granted the status of existence, so now I will remain neutral on the subject. It seems that relations are predicated on the existence of objects.[16] Relation should be the second category in the ontological table.

Consider three extra directions in which to expand the preliminary description of relations. First, return to the simple portrayal of space–time as a coordinate lattice, with either an object existing or not at each coordinate.[17] Imagine that relations may encode not only between any two objects, but also may encode among any number of objects. For example, one object can be "between" two other objects, for a three-place relation. Relations, therefore, are polyadic, described by several terms to encode among any number of objects.[18] With enough smallest objects encoded in a relation we may encode a mountain, that is, describe a macroscopic physical thing. Macroscopic objects then are bound patterns of relations among the smallest objects.[19] Second, since objects may have the characteristic of either existing or not existing, then a relation can relate among existent objects and nonexistent objects—that is, maybe thought of as an empty coordinate in space–time. Like 1s and 0s in a multidimensional array in computer software, existence and nonexistence can together encode information. Any particular collection of objects need not exist to allow encoding of a well-formed relation. Third, this ontology is described within the context of a space–time manifold, and there is a temporal dimension. Relations may also encode among objects (existing and nonexisting) through time. Relations so elaborated provide a broad descriptive power. Because the *relata* can be existent or nonexistent objects, existing or not existing through time, relations are fairly unconstrained, permitting relations that can encode Quine's (1969) possible fat man standing in a doorway,[20] or a winged Pegasus flying from Kripke's mind's eye to our own.

I offer an inclusive description of relations, encompassing all the kinds of relations encountered in philosophical discussion. Relations can encode among any number of objects, with the objects either existent or nonexistent in space, and with such objects in the relation found (or not found) at any time. A large percentage of these relations will be trivial or nonsensical. As examples, think of some relation between a molecule of ammonia on Jupiter and the period at the end of this sentence, or between the author William Faulkner and a winged Pegasus. Notice that "William Faulkner" refers to a previously existing person, the collection of particles existent at a particular place in the past. "Pegasus" refers to a mythological creature, a collection of particles nonexistent in space–time, imagined by ancient Greeks, with that relation promulgated by other relations—various arrangements of letters recorded in books—to our own time. The main use for these relations not among real physical objects is that some can encode information—which you can readily hold as a thought in your head—arranged in true analytic statements.

The table of ontological categories now provisionally contains two elements, objects and relations, granting existence to objects and a neutral status to relations. If the physical universe is finite, then there exists a finite number of objects at any one time. If time is finite, then there are a finite number of objects existing over time. If both time and the universe are finite, then there are a finite number of smallest objects (one ontological category) in a finite universe, with relations encoding information (a second ontological category).[21]

I now address a third element originated in classical philosophical thought and in common conversation, namely 'properties', to ask whether properties are a necessary element in the ontological table. Philosophers credit two main characteristics to properties, as <u>having causative powers</u>, and as <u>being truthmakers</u>. Either properties need be added to the ontological table, or these necessary roles need to be carried out by other ontological elements.

Where are the Properties?

Physicists use their instrumentation to explore microscopic scales, providing evidence for hypothesizing what elements might constitute the universe. The evidence does not favor continued use of properties as primary constitutive elements, as illustrated with a simple thought experiment.

Imagine peering into the microscopic world, examining ever-smaller objects in search of the smallest real object. The focus moves to objects smaller than organic cells (at about 10^{-5} m), to visible light waves (from 400 nm to 700 nm, or 10^{-6} m), molecules (about 10^{-10} m), to the size of an average atomic nucleus (at 1.6–15 fm, or about 10^{-14} m for an average atom) (Metcalf, Williams, & Castka, 1980, p. 43). A single proton in an atomic nucleus is about 1 fm (10^{-15} m) in size. The three quarks[22] that compose a proton are about 10^{-18} m. A neutrino is generally considered as or close to a point particle, with its mass estimated at less than 0.086 eV, or a size smaller than 10^{-24} m (Loureiro, Arthur et al., 2019). The possible "quantum foam," likely is of the Planck length of 10^{-35} m.[23] The Heisenberg uncertainty principle[24] applies to scales above the Planck limits. Below the Planck scale the momenta and energies become nonsensical (very large), and the current theory fails in its explanation.

The brief review of scale for microscopic and smaller objects is a preamble to dissect the philosophical thinking behind properties. We tend to focus most readily on secondary properties, properties that we can experience, such as color. In philosophical history, it was thought that these "inhere in" objects. Aristotle (1984) couched the discussion in terms of primary substances and secondary substances, with primary substances as fundamental ontological elements, and those as necessary for any secondary substances (2a35-2b7). The current use of the term properties parallels Aristotle's argument. I will argue that the secondary properties as measured scientifically do not point to anything inhering in objects. Further, the primary properties as measured scientifically need not be thought of as properties, but instead may be thought of as relations. The elegance of fundamental equations of physics lies in the relationships between fundamental properties or, simply, as relations. For example, Einstein's equation, $E = mc^2$, demonstrates the relations Energy = (mass)(length)^2 /(time)^2; and momentum = (mass)(length) /(time). There is no lack of examples.

In light of the scientific study of small scales, consider trying to locate the primary and secondary properties[25] traditionally described by philosophy. Secondary properties include properties of sensations, such as color, taste, smell, and sound. Primary properties include the properties of motion, solidity, extension, mass, and number. An updated list would likely include primary property terms, such as electrical charge, spin, and color charge, given to certain subatomic particles.

Notice that the secondary quality of visible color does not exist at smaller than the scale of visible light (about 10^{-6} m) because reflected light brings about the sensation of color. Taste and smell disappear below the molecular scale (about 10^{-10} m) because the relation among atoms in molecules is necessary to excite sensations in an organism's perceptual apparatus. Sound also disappears below the molecular scale because sound propagates as waves through a molecular medium. Turning to the primary properties, motion is a function of relative molecular movement. Solidity is a function of the Pauli Exclusion Principle and electromagnetic forces (Eisberg & Resnick, 1985, p. 337). Below the scale of about 10^{-15} m, these primary properties also disappear.[26] Mathematical models in physics posit "particles," which lack the property of dimension. Some of the smallest elements in current models lack mass.[27] The mental experiment suggests scales below which nearly all[28] of the traditional exemplar secondary and primary properties are no longer manifest. These are scales describing a physical world, a world of objects, scaling down to the smallest conceivable physical object. With the move to smaller scales, explicitly shedding relations, the putative properties disappear. Yet evidence of any elements that *are* the properties have never been found. Scientific probing at microscopic levels raises the question of whether properties even exist. At a minimum, properties do not exist "inside" other objects as commonly used in our talk. This may be true even about the smallest conceivable objects since the explanatory use for properties fails at every level to which instrumentation has given science access. In current physics, within the dimensions of space–time, there seems little conclusive evidence for an independent ontological category consistent with a "property."

Redefining Relations, to Do More Work

In a table of ontological elements, if properties are eliminated, then the two main characteristics attributed to them need be carried by some other element. I argue these roles can be done by relations.

I recognize that a primary hurdle to accepting this claim is our strong intuitions about causality, and the feeling that relations "don't do anything." To overcome this (incorrect, I claim) intuition, several more steps are needed. This intuition is because the label 'relation' commingles two roles, one with causal powers, the second without. Let's take a step to remove this tangle.

I propose a distinction identifying two nonhierarchical classes of relations, to split the inclusive description of relations now in use. The first class distinguishes causative powers and truth-making in nature. The second class further elaborates on a basis for other truth-making characteristics attributed to properties. To the distinction: what philosophers have called 'relations' really consist of two elements, as different as lightning and thunder. I suggest the old inclusive 'relations' consist of *physically causative relations* (PCRs) and *non-causative relations* (NCRs), with most of the latter having no significance grounded in the physical reality of the universe.[29]

First to the lightning, to be more precise about PCRs. There are many such relations, and they may tell us something about how the natural world is organized. For objects (e.g., particles) linked as *relata* by such relations, the relations describe causal powers at work. Certain of the *relata* are proximate to one another in space–time. Adjacent atoms form molecular bonds. Philosophers may construct a relation ("one molecule of water is 'bound to' another molecule of water") or describe a property ("there is a property of 'molecular bonding' at work among water molecules"). Certain adjacent molecules form relationships that characterize the surface tension on a drop of water, or the solidity of a table surface. Many PCRs are between objects separated in space. For example, the laws of physics say a force of gravitational attraction exists between Earth and the planet Neptune. This can be described traditionally as a property (the property of gravitational attraction acting between two bodies), or better as a relation (in a sentence, "Earth is 'gravitationally attracted to' Neptune"), or scientifically as a field (a relation among many particles in space–time). The fields favored by physicists can be described as relational to the smallest scales.[30] Some partial theories of quantum gravity suggest that relations among elements are causal at the scale of the fabric of space–time.[31] These few examples suggest a generalization, that PCRs are causative (thus the name). If so, this class of relations "carves nature at its joints" (Plato, Phaedrus,

265e) and thereby describes natural laws. Then PCRs also can be truthmakers. In this role, truth is measured by the correctness of the relation to describe a causative power among the apparent objects we perceive in the physical world.

Second to the thunder. While NCRs do not physically cause anything, some can act as information carriers, similar to the truth-making role in nature for PCRs. Philosophers argue that properties can be truthmakers[32] in a sentence. If philosophy is to rely only on relations without properties, then the truth of any predication should come about because of the obtaining of a relation, rather than through possession of a monadic property. Then the truth of the predication is grounded by the truth of the relation, either because it relates *relata* existent in the world, or it relates existent and nonexistent *relata* in identity relationships or in logical relationships.[33] More precisely, I propose that an NCR may be a truthmaker in three cases. First, a relation may be a truthmaker for which all its *relata* are grounded objects, or in relations which are ultimately grounded in objects. (The true sentence "Denver is in Colorado" is an example. Note that the relation itself is not causing anything so is not a PCR.) Second, a relation that forms an identity relationship among existent or nonexistent *relata* is a truthmaker. (An example of grounded objects is the true sentence "an elephant is larger than a bacterium." An example for non-grounded objects is the true sentence "unicorns have horns," for which the subject is nonexistent.) Third, a relation that follows the rules of logic may be a truthmaker, admitting logical and mathematical statements. The distinction between PCRs and NCRs calls special attention to existent causative elements in the physically closed universe. Yet it also gives the truth-making role to relations, accounting for truth-making in nature and through ways that truth may be carried in information. The distinction splits truth-making between two separate ontological elements.

What can be interpreted as a failed counterexample from Fodor (1988, p. 33) may (unintentionally for him) illustrate my approach both to causative powers and to truth-making. Fodor believed in a profusion of properties. He proposed to define for a particle the property of *being an H-particle* just in case it is a particle and a coin tossed by Fodor lands heads. (Note that Fodor's *H-particle* has nothing to do with the element hydrogen.) One interpretation is that *being an H-particle* is simply a 'Cambridge property,' or one in which nothing is added to individuals; but this interpretation still uses the language of properties. Instead, PCRs and NCRs can explain it. Fodor's H-particle appears to be a relation that bridges among (1) his hand, (2) a coin, and (3) the outcome of the event of Fodor's tossing the coin with (4) the idea of an H-particle (which itself is a NCR, of a nonexistent particle). While the first three relations are all grounded in the physical world, the fourth is not, nor is there any PCR in nature that may be associated with it (as corroborated, for example, by scientific testing). The lack of grounding for the imaginary H-particle explains our correct intuition that no overall truthmaker is at work. The relation labeled an 'H-particle' is not causative, again because it is not completely constituted of PCRs. (Fodor's hand tossing the coin is physically causative, but that is a different relation than the one labeled with the property of *being an H-particle*.) This analysis suggests that there is no property of *being an H-particle*. In the replacement terminology, there is no PCR for an H-particle.[34] More generally, the distinction between lightning (PCRs, causative elements in the world, and truthmakers in nature) and thunder (NCRs which may be truthmakers if obeying certain rules, and which are meaningless relations if not truthmakers) yields no need for properties.

PCRs Doing the Work of Causal Powers

Note again that properties traditionally fulfill the role of <u>having causative powers</u>. A second thought experiment examines using relations to replace properties in this role. Imagine the collision between a large truck and a bicycle. From experience we expect the bicycle will lose in such a crash; the truck will smash the bicycle. How might this physically causative event be characterized ontologically? Likely few would describe the encounter using the language of properties at the macroscopic level, to say the result is a "property of largeness" on the part of the truck. More likely would be to use an explanation from physics, to say the truck and bicycle are composed of molecules (for example, constituting steel, rubber), that molecular bonds hold the molecules together into two relative collections of particles, that the collections of particles have momentum proportional to the velocity times the mass of each collection, and that mathematics (quantity and direction of momentum of particles) generally dictates where the molecules will end up. Then one may be tempted to talk about the "property of inertial mass." Such a property is nothing inherent to any object, but instead, is itself born of a relationship. Inertial mass, the mass of an object measured by resistance to acceleration, may be defined (beginning with Newton's second law, $F = ma$), in relation to a reference object. Then the inertial mass of object x, compared to reference object y, might be defined by $m_x/m_y = a_y/a_x$. Inertial mass might also be described in relation to gravity via the principle of equivalence, $m_g = m_i$. In either case, properties need not enter the description, and PCRs suffice. One can trace a chain of relations, from relations among molecules, to relations among the atoms composing molecules, to the relations among constituents of atoms, down to the smallest reaches of instrumentation. Therefore, given the current scientific data, it seems that PCRs may do the work of causality usually attributed to properties.

A Metaphysical Handstand

The argument discards properties as a separate element in the ontological table. I claim that relations can do all the work assigned to properties, if a distinction is made between PCRs and NCRs, to sort out the physically causative and truth-making roles. The ontological table of elements with these changes would provisionally consist of PCRs, NCRs, and objects.

My purpose is to provide physicists and philosophers with a simple ontological framework, better reflecting the world, to change the manner of speaking and thinking.[35] I employed a rational[36] argument to arrive at a provisional ontological table of elements. The supporting logic holds even if we now look at the argument in a radically different way. I shall now flip our view of the ontological structure on its head (and facing backward) in a metaphysical handstand,[37] turning to further evidence from the physical sciences. The argument becomes more concrete and physical.

To describe the physical universe at the finest scale, one might imagine a lattice structure of points and connective edges, corresponding to objects and relations, respectively. In our typical ontological perspective, causation is associated with objects. What if we flipped both ways of thinking simultaneously, that of the objects and relations, and that of causality? This would be a metaphysical handstand, an inversion in two dimensions. I propose first that the ontological table should consist of relations and objects, with *relations having existence and provisional neutrality about the existence of objects*. These relations really exist, with the points as markers designating the places where relations meet. For example, there may exist many relations associated with a particular point. There may be a relation between A and Z, another between B and Z, and another between C and Z. Second, I propose that the PCRs are physically causative. Third, we perceive none of these relations as entities because they exist in another dimension, not in our perceivable dimensions of space–time.

Reality is composed of however-many dimensions there actually are, an empirical question. Our best physics, a physics of real things, says that there are more dimensions than those we know of space and time, and all those dimensions exist in this one universe. The mathematics suggests those extra dimensions are there, even if we can't access them. Then what is real must exist within those dimensions, which means some machinery could hide in dimensions to which we have no

A METAPHYSICAL ONTOLOGY CONSISTING ONLY OF RELATIONS

access. Only one extra dimension is needed in which to hide the relations. If the hypothesis is true, then the mathematics explaining the universe should center on causative relations.[38]

We cannot locate anything like a property by searching down through the size scales in the physically measurable world. We cannot find the causes. For physicists, the state of physics is like engineers trying to describe the operation of an internal combustion engine when the electrical system somehow exists in a different spatial dimension from the rest of the machine. The pistons move in their cylinders. Exactly when a piston reaches the top of each cylinder, at an exact point in space, a spark appears from somewhere and the exploding gases drive the piston down. If the electrical system is invisible in our three spatial and one temporal dimension, the underlying cause (electricity moving from the battery via wires to spark plug) is hidden. The engineers may infer a cause, and reliably predict the engine's turning through time, but they can only point to the relations among the engine's components for an explanation.

Like the engineers measuring the spark from the spark plug (when the causative electrical system is hidden), so physicists measure energy and mass at a point in space–time, seeming to come from a particle. Worse than for the engineers analyzing their engine, I am suggesting that the universal engine hides in another dimension, with only the intersections of causes appearing in space–time. The appearance of energy and mass, position and momentum, are byproducts of the hidden relational web. If this is true, then what we notice in space–time are not the hidden existent relations, but rather the objects (points) where relations come together.

With the metaphysical roles (of objects and relations) reversed from the provisional description, it follows that these objects or points need not really exist. Then objects may be epiphenomenal. With all our scientific instruments, what we measure as an electron may not be something with physical existence. Then we should say about objects (points, particles) that there is "no there there." This hypothesis offers the notion that atoms, and all the particles composing them, may not exist in the way that we have conceived of them for the past hundred years.[39]

We see a red apple and reach out to hold it. We imagine our hand, comprising molecules, acting on another grouping of molecules that compose the apple. Physics says the feeling of firmness is because of atomic forces that cause atoms to press back against atoms. What if we abandon the mental model of a physical atomic entity existing in space–time? Instead we might imagine an arrangement of relations that compose the apple, and an arrangement of relations that compose our hand, with the act of grasping the apple a causal relation of the latter relations acting on the former. The points where causative relations meet only appear to have effects in space–time. These are the points where PCRs in the hidden dimension(s) intersect with space–time. The nonhierarchical[40] flux of causative relations would manifest all the same observable effects—particles, organized into other particles, organized into atoms (all variously measurable with instruments), organized into the physical world that we can perceive.

Now imagine that we open our hand and the apple falls to the ground. Experience and science since Newton provide an explanation for *how* gravity works. The child's question is *where* is gravity? The ontological question is *what* is gravity? A response is that gravity exists in a hidden dimension, and that gravity is a web of PCRs.

New Ontological Labels

My major ontological concern is with *what there is*—what things there are that have *existence*. I have employed the language labels *objects*, *properties*, and *relations* generally as they have been used in philosophy and in common discussion, as a bridge to be understandable. We can only ascribe meaning to what we can understand. The label *relation* carries certain meanings that have obfuscated the multiple unrelated mean-

A METAPHYSICAL ONTOLOGY CONSISTING ONLY OF RELATIONS

ings for which it has been used. To sort out meaning, I've used the terms PCR and NCR to describe two flavors of relations, and to better identify them as entirely different elements.

These several steps have been taken to help us think about the universe in a different way. That is the rationale to use the clumsy terms PCR and NCR, two labels to bridge an impediment. Because we are embedded in the universe and know it via our perceptual apparatus, it is nearly impossible not to think about it using a simplistic Newtonian model of particles in motion, with particles causing other particles to move about. We've reinforced this perception since infancy. I hope to overcome this mental barrier, to ignore the wrong view that objects are causative, and to embrace the view instead that the pattern, the relation is causative.

Given our perceptual blinders, the way for us to think about what is real is to use what we can imagine as real. By analogy, I will describe something you may imagine to be real, say a lightning bolt, curved around so the ends touch. Imagine the lightning bolt is in one of the other dimensions that physicists believe exist beyond space–time. That lightning bolt, that PCR, is what I want you to imagine is real. Where the ends of the PCR come together, imagine that there we find something working in space–time, maybe some quark of our existence, even if that thing is epiphenomenal and does not really exist. Second, when lightning strikes, we anticipate the boom that follows, something that we interpret as not really affecting the world in the same manner, but still existent.

Let me replace the PCR and NCR by more elegant terminology. Rather than PCR, we might label this instead as a **bolt**. Think of it as an element that connects points in a space–time lattice, where the bolt is the source of causality. Second, let me replace NCR by the label **boom**. Booms are non-causative information carriers, and the implications of their existence[41] are left for another time. It's relations all the way down.[42]

With this last step of providing labels for ontological elements to shed a great deal of metaphysical baggage, we arrive at the ontological table. The proposed ontology, a bolt hypothesis, consists of two elements, bolt and boom. There is no need for objects. The common thinking that objects exist in the world is abandoned, and such appearance are epiphenomena.

A Further Analogy to Make the "Real" Real

Perhaps my reader has looked up from this page with a dawning idea of a new way to see the closed physical universe which we inhabit. More likely, with eyes glazing over after wandering from the prior paragraphs, the words pass meaningless through a mind grounded firmly in its perception of the world, and bolts and booms remain devoid of any meaning. It is near impossible to pry one's mind from this perception. We clutch our "real" reading material as we stare up from the page. We believe there must be something like 'properties' embedded in real objects surrounding us. Now reader, now scientist, now philosopher, now seeker, I urge you to try again to see the world anew. If you are successful, the thunderbolt will strike you. The hollow keystone of properties will be broken, and the impossible edifice will fall.

I'm asking you again to try to imagine that the relations are real, and that the objects we perceive are mere shadows of the relations.

What Hume said about excessive skeptical arguments can be doubly said about any attempt to unroot our minds from the perceptual model with which they have been trained since our first perception:

> These may flourish and triumph in the schools; where it is, indeed, difficult, if not impossible, to refute them. But as soon as they leave the shade, and by the presence of the real objects, which actuate our passions and sentiments, are put in opposition to the more powerful principles of our nature,

A METAPHYSICAL ONTOLOGY CONSISTING ONLY OF RELATIONS

they vanish like smoke, and leave the most determined sceptic in the same condition as other mortals. (Hume, 1907, p. 169)

I recognize that my claim is a David against the perceptual Goliath of "real objects," which we may only push away to understand the underlying reality for brief moments. There is no language now in use to say what I want to say. But for a patient reader, let me try one more time to make the argument. Let me summarize the logic of the argument, and then provide one more analogy.

I use a rationalist approach favored by Cartesians, using the power of thought to find the truth, in which I examine possible basic ontological elements. I ask the rhetorical question, "Where are properties?" The conclusion, based on a physics gedankenexperiment, is there is no place for them to be found. My initial conclusion is that one might get by with only objects and relations, if some elements might do the work ascribed to properties, namely, as having causative powers and as truthmakers. My claim is that relations can do both. But two new terms for 'relations' are needed. The new terms are bolts, for physically causative relations, and booms for non-causative relations. The former property roles are not mapped one-to-one to the new terms, because the role of truthmaker is performed by both bolts and booms.

If bolts and booms do perform the roles of having causative powers and as truthmakers, then the conclusion following from the formulation is that objects are unnecessary as ontological elements. Bolts and booms really exist in a physically closed universe, and those describe everything. Relations are patterns; the universe is a pattern.

The mental leap needed to embrace this model is to imagine that some sort of relation can be causative. It is an upside-down and backward view—a metaphysical handstand.

Now to one more analogy. Elsewhere[48] I described a mental model, the "block universe," to better envision space–time as being of a piece as implied by special relativity. In that model, space–time is imagined in three dimensions. But we can carry the exercise one step farther. Imagine three-dimensional space as represented by one dimension, and time as a second dimension. Then space–time is a plane in an infinite universe, and perhaps imagined as a plane folded into a sphere for a finite universe. As we imagine the sphere of space–time, we can readily recognize room for further dimensions, namely, "inside" the sphere and "outside" the sphere. These are analogous to the six or seven extra dimensions (for a total of ten or eleven) that current physics guesses most likely describe our real, closed physical universe. My suggestion is that the mechanism of causative bolts might be hidden away in one of the dimensions outside space–time, outside the sphere. Imagine a Zeus holding a lattice of bolts, bending them so the ends touch the surface of the sphere. The bolts are causative, with the result of that causation appearing on the surface of the sphere. I suggest that those bolts, those patterns, are the root of causation perceived in space–time. They create the perception of real objects. I suggest that Zeus is also us.

3 Viewpoint on Certain Puzzles Given a Simplified Ontology

Why this radically different way to arrange the ontological furniture? The bolt hypothesis removes certain ontological ideas and associated philosophical terminology that has been demonstrated by scientific experimentation to be wrong. It offers as replacement a simple table of ontological elements that describe a physical universe. It offers insight into several empirical discoveries that have puzzled physics and philosophy for some time. Let me offer a comment on our view of the universe informed by the bolt hypothesis, followed by five examples from science and philosophy where the hypothesis may suggest new ways to approach certain outstanding questions.

A Universe Not of Empty Space, But Instead a Rich Pattern

The bolt hypothesis proposes a new view of the universe. The view from the metaphysical handstand would reverse the idea that the universe has vast empty spaces at the smallest and largest scales.[44]

At the atomic scale, non-quantum models suggested that most of the volume of an atom is taken up by empty space, since the diameter of a simple atom is of the order of 10^{-10} m, compared to the diameter of a nucleon at about 10^{-15} m. Using modern quantum-mechanical models, in the simplest hydrogen atom (with one electron and one proton) as an example, the electron exists as a spherical cloud of probability. According to the Copenhagen interpretation of quantum theory, the probability is resolved into a position only with a measurement, and interaction of the particle with a measuring device. These and other subatomic particles are widely spaced, oases in a desert, and mysterious in their existence.

At galactic scales, the astronomically close Andromeda galaxy, which is part of the Local Group with the Milky Way galaxy, is 2.5 million light-years distant, or about 2.4×10^{22} m. The visible universe[45] is on the order of 10^{26} m or 10^{27} m. We imagine that the "empty" space between galaxies is a hard vacuum of low-density particles, with subatomic particles continuously coming into and out of existence.[46] Conventional quantum physics says the vacuum is teaming with activity, containing particles, dark matter, and dark energy, yet all at very low densities.

From smallest to largest scales, the current picture is of a desert universe, incredibly vast with widely scattered tiny bits of matter.

If instead we accept that bolts are real, existing in another dimension at the Planck scale, then the universe is a dense entity, a tightly bound web of bolts. It would not have any low-density space in between. Like an artist seeing the spaces between the lines, the reverse view of the universe is much richer.

Bolts and Wave-Particle Duality via Double-Slit Experiments

The double-slit experiment apparently demonstrates that matter and energy can display characteristics of both waves and particles. The experiment has been done with a coherent light source (a laser beam), with photons, neutrons, electrons, and molecules. In the first configuration, the beam illuminates a thin plate with two slits, and a detector is placed behind the plate. The light passing through the two slits interferes to produce dark and light bands at the detector. The light and dark bands appear to result from waves and troughs, adding and canceling, consistent with light waves passing through the two slits and forming an interference pattern. The light at the detector is absorbed as if it resulted from discrete particles (photons). Experiments have been conducted with the beam consisting of single particles emitted, and individual particles are detected at the plate (displaying a particle nature). But in the pattern built up over time, the interference pattern can be found. The result appears as if each particle passed through both slits and interfered with itself. The evidence opposes normal intuitions about locality of particles, and temporal relationships among separate events. It is counterintuitive that whether we get a particle pattern (if we successfully measure which slit the particle went through), or a wave interference pattern (if we don't successfully measure which slit the particle went through) depends on whether we are successful in making a measurement.

The current theory offers no consensus explanation for the evidence. Rovelli (1996) offered a relational explanation, that a relation is formed between the particles under observation and the detector. His explanation contradicts the intuition that we do not find macroscopic objects, such as the detector device, causally intertwined with particles on the lowest scales.

The bolt hypothesis also suggests there is not a particle existing in space–time at the detector. The detector is another web of bolts, arranged in a particular configuration. The measurement (in space–time) records the result of the interaction of many bolts, with the resultant 'particle' designating the endpoints or markers for bolts. The detector is fine-tuned to interact with the bolts representing the 'particle.' That particular pattern of bolts could engender the different measurement results.[47]

Bolts and Nonlocality

One riddle arising from quantum theory might be partially explained if the reality available to our perception, via our senses and our instrumentation, lacks intrinsic properties "in" objects in space–time. This is the quandary posed by tests of Bell's inequalities, and more recently refined by tests of Leggett's inequalities. The experiments have baffled physicists because the results defy explanation within the framework of real particles imbued with intrinsic properties. The best explanation by physics is that they are quantum superpositions of properties.

Restated slightly, the major question raised is whether particles in a quantum state possess local properties. Quantum theory says that paired electrons are described by a single wave function until measured. For configurations of paired particles separated in space, quantum theory violates the idea that particles are real entities containing all their properties. Einstein deeply disagreed with the quantum theory conclusion and continued to believe in the local realism of particles (that is, particles existing at a point in space–time). The EPR[48] argument in 1935 suggested that quantum theory is incomplete and that some additional variables are necessary to account for locality and causality. In 1964, Bell offered a method to test for local realism, with an argument that directly challenged the EPR paper's conclusion (Bell, 1964). Bell's theorem is based around a set of measurable inequalities. In contrast to Einstein's view, Bell's theorem suggests that if Bell's inequalities are violated, then no physical theory of local hidden variables[49] can reproduce all the predictions of quantum theory. The concept of a hidden variable is similar to that of a property—for example, the property of spin-up possessed by a particle. If Bell's inequalities are violated in quantum experiments, then it would suggest there are not hidden variables that inhere in the physical object represented by a particle in a particular location.

In experiments conducted by Aspect and others (Aspect, Dalibard, & Roger, 1982), Bell's inequalities were found to be violated. Such experiments to test Bell's inequalities may begin with paired photons, sent in opposite directions. The polarization of each photon may be detected by two-channel polarizers. The instrumentation is oriented at various 'Bell test angles' and the state of the photons tabulated. The number of coincidences for various angles is compared with the values predicted by quantum theory to determine whether Bell's inequalities are violated. Multiple experiments have been conducted to reconfirm the results and to close possible loopholes,[50] such as the "detection loophole" (when particles are not all detected on both parts of the experiment), the "locality loophole" or "communication loophole" (ensuring that the quantum process used was random, generally by sufficiently separating the objects at the time of measurement), and the "efficiency loophole" (guaranteeing that a fair sample was obtained). The weight of evidence confirms that Bell's inequalities are violated, and that quantum theory is vindicated.[51]

Leggett's inequalities take a further step to separate nonlocality from reality (Leggett, 2003). Experiments were conducted by Gröblacher, Aspelmeyer, Zeilinger, and others to test Liggett's inequalities, and these were also shown to be violated (Gröblacher, et al., 2007). The conclusion from the experiments is that hidden variables not only are not local, but also that they do not inhere in the "real" particles. Together, the experiments testing Bell's inequalities and Leggett's inequalities suggest there are no hidden variables—and no prop-

A METAPHYSICAL ONTOLOGY CONSISTING ONLY OF RELATIONS

erties—inhering in the "real" objects that we have heretofore characterized as particles.

The bolt hypothesis offers a possible insight into the dilemma posed by the Bell and Leggett inequality experiments. While the violations of the Bell and Leggett inequalities rule out all local hidden variable theories, they do not rule out nonlocal sources for quantum entanglement. My solution is a variant on a nonlocal variable, via the mechanism of a bolt. First assume that the particles being tested are not real, local particles, but rather represent the points where relations (existing in another dimension) meet. Then there is nothing magical about particles changing properties (since there are no such intrinsic local variables); nor would there be anything magical about particles coming into existence or going out of existence as viewed by our instruments in space–time. Physicists need instead to discover the rules governing interactions among bolts that would cause these observed outcomes in space–time (albeit, a difficult problem, like that facing the engineers with the nonobservable engine). The perspectival change is to not search for some rationale "in" the (nonexistent) particle, but to imagine what web of bolts, operating in another dimension, might be the collective cause of the observed phenomena in space–time. Bolts act collectively as a web,[52] not individually as points or particles.

Many bolts, then, might interact in ways resulting in the appearance of points of causation that scientific instruments identify as particles. Most trace out tracks in space–time and appear with consistent characteristics that are interpreted as intrinsic properties. But some bolts may not interact with such a result, and these outliers can reveal the true nature of reality. Using current terminology, the Bell and Leggett inequality violations suggest that two particles separated in space do not acquire a particular property until some later time when something else happens (a measurement). In contrast, we should imagine that the two separated particles, and the measuring instrumentation, all "really" are bolts in an interrelated bolt web acting in a hidden dimension. The particular web of bolts aligns in a way to manifest the appearance of a particular property (for example, spin-up) centered at one point in space–time (i.e., appearing in one particle) with the complement appearing at another point in space–time (in the paired particle). Through this mechanism, the apparent paired properties appear in our measuring instruments. In this model, there is something ontologically real underpinning this scientific realism, yet the elements that are real are bolts existent in the universe (space–time plus hidden dimensions) but not found in space–time.

If the view from the metaphysical handstand is the correct one, a way is open to explain measurements of violations of the Bell and Leggett inequalities. Then the particles supposedly appearing in our instruments do not really exist. The problems facing physicists are even greater because the entire machinery of causation is hidden. But by embracing a new perspective, new experiments may be proposed that hypothesize possible arrangements of bolts that would result in the observed phenomena. Mathematical models will continue to direct experimental inquiry, but maybe along new avenues.

Mental Causation and Mentality

Perhaps the most baffling problem in philosophy of mind is the problem of mental causation within a physically closed universe. Jaegwon Kim offered a forceful statement of the problem. Kim poses the question, "How is it possible for the mind to exercise its causal powers in a world that is fundamentally physical?" If the mind is not causal, then the ideas we hold about human volition are an illusion. I will refer to his formulation of the most significant problem, the problem of causal exclusion.

In the philosophy of mind, supervenience has been invoked as a minimal condition for causality that meets the physicalist requirement for closure under the physical universe. Supervenience is a set of dependency relationships held between properties of the mind (M) and the physical substrate of the brain (P). The catchphrase for the mental supervenience relationship is, "There cannot be an M-difference without a P-difference." Said more formally, the set of M-properties supervene upon P-properties just in case no two things can differ with respect to M-properties without also differing with respect to their P-properties.

Assume two mental events, one temporally causing the next, with their associated physical instantiations. If we are to believe that our mental states cause temporally related mental states, then m (some prior mental event) must be a cause of m*. We also suppose that mental event m* of mental kind M causes physical event p* of physical kind P. To meet the physical causal closure constraint,[53] physical event p* must have been caused by some prior temporal event p. But since physical event p causes p*, then p* has two causes, both m* and p. We see that p* is over-determined, and there seems to be no real work for mental event m* to do. Kim says that "if mind-body supervenience fails, there is no visible way of understanding the possibility of mental causation" (2002, p. 175). If one accepts supervenience, and accepts the causal closure of the physical universe, then the causal relationships (between m and p, m* and p*) must hold. But the causality relationships resulting from M-P supervenience are not a sufficient condition to avoid epiphenomenalism. What is a physicalist to do? Should we join in Fodor's lament (Fodor J. A., p. 156), and conclude that all is lost, including our human agency and the possibility of human knowledge, and "it's the end of the world"?

Elsewhere[54] I provide a fuller refutation of this conclusion. Here note that Kim's argument is couched in the language of properties and property causation. The bolt hypothesis says that properties do not exist. If there are no properties, and instead causality is due to bolts, and if mentality itself is composed of bolts, then the problem evaporates: mentality is directly causative.

Bolts, Indeterminism, and Free Will

Within philosophy, one of the most profound open questions is whether we have free will. Let me suggest that if a physically closed universe is governed by indeterminacy, and if mentality itself consists of bolts, then we can have free will. I will elaborate the argument by reviewing some definitions for free will, by mentioning evidence from physics that suggests the universe is governed by indeterminism, and then examine the resulting inferences and the question of free will.

We may begin with some accepted definitions of free will. As one minimal definition, "[F]ree will is the ability to select a course of action as a means of fulfilling some desire" (O'Connor, 2009, p. 3). Beyond this minimum, most philosophers have required a further authorship, with the agent as the ultimate originator of action. Aristotle said, "... when the origin of the actions is in him, it is also up to him to do them or not to do them" (O'Connor, 2009, p. 2). We find here a two-millennium-old notion of free will that incorporates "could have done otherwise."[55] Many philosophers include in free will an "agent causation" in which "the agent himself causes his choice or action, and this is not to be reductively analyzed as an event within the agent causing the choice" (O'Connor, 2009, p. 14).

These are robust definitions of free will that go beyond an ability to do something randomly different. The freedom to do something randomly different, mere volatility, does not offer a free will worth having, because randomness does not provide authorship.[56]

No such free will is possible in a fully deterministic universe. One definition of determinism we may use is, "The world is governed by (or is under the sway of) determinism if and only if, given a specified way things are at a time t, the way things go thereafter is fixed as a matter of natural law" (Hoefer, 2010, p. 2).

For free will to be possible, indeterminacy must describe the universe. Max Jammer defined three meanings of indeterminacy (1973, p. 586). Indeterminacy may denote (1) an es-

A METAPHYSICAL ONTOLOGY CONSISTING ONLY OF RELATIONS

sential limitation or *imprecision* of measurement procedures, (2) any type of *unpredictable* behavior of physical processes without necessarily involving a renunciation of metaphysical causality, and (3) any type of *acausal* (accidental, contingent, or indeterministic) behavior of physical processes, usually in the realm of microphenomena, implying a total breakdown of the principle of causality. For free will to be possible, then the latter two types of indeterminacy should be found, beyond merely science's incapacity to measure.

Let me suggest that the advent of modern science opened with an intellectual acceptance of scientific determinism to describe the universe, but that during the past century that view has been overturned by evidence for indeterminacy. With the eighteenth-century acceptance of Newtonian physics, a deterministic clockwork universe became the default view. Laplace offered his 'intellect' or demon articulating this scientific determinism. The idea was that if someone (a demon, perhaps a stand-in for God) could know the exact location and momentum of every particle in the universe, then all past and future values are entailed. Einstein's GR and QM unseated the Newtonian view. Laplace's demon has been defeated by several directed arguments and arguably by the discovery of a new field of mathematics. One argument against the demon is that it would require 10^{120} bits of information, more than the universe holds (Lloyd, August 2000). Second, a mathematical proof (a Cantor diagonalization) shows that, if the demon is a computational device, no two such devices can completely predict each other (Wolpert, 2008).

Maybe a stronger assault on (at least, on the determinism implied by) Laplace's demon comes from the mathematical field of chaos theory and complex systems. The theory is supported by countless discoveries of complex systems in nature. These systems are highly sensitive to initial conditions, making them unpredictable per Jammer's second definition for indeterminacy. While complexity science does not completely defeat Laplace's demon *per se* (because by assumption it possesses perfect knowledge), they do argue that the causality rules governing the universe make it unpredictable, and that this fact is fundamental to the manner that it operates. Complex systems define nature rather than the more conventional view that most of the world has some predictability. (The common view may be a result of evolutionary selection that conserved the ability to track patterns, aiding survivability; therefore, we see the patterns and ignore the chaos.)

When quantum physics replaced the Newtonian interpretation, another indeterminacy was found to describe the universe. Studying quantum mechanics of fundamental particles in 1927, Werner Heisenberg introduced the Heisenberg position–momentum uncertainty relation (or indeterminacy principle), which says that *it is impossible to measure simultaneously both the position and the momentum of a quantum-mechanical system with arbitrary accuracy; the more precise the measurement of one of these two variables is, the less precise is that of the other.* It is not the result of mere measurement limitations, but rather that the concepts of exact position and velocity together have no meaning in nature. The indeterminacy principle is inherent in all wavelike quantum systems. These quantum systems exhibit acausal indeterminacy behavior per Jammer's definition.

Quantum indeterminacy was early seen as challenging the determinism precluding free will. Eddington said, "If the atom has indeterminacy, surely the human mind will have an equal indeterminacy; for we can scarcely accept a theory which makes out the mind to be more mechanistic than the atom" (1932, pp. 66-80). This indeterminacy is not limited to quantum effects, for

> "So it is often claimed that although quantum mechanics seems to imply indeterminism and single-case probabilities, these can be confined to the microscopic level. Plainly, however, if there is indeterminism among quantum events and there is any

A METAPHYSICAL ONTOLOGY CONSISTING ONLY OF RELATIONS

coupling of them to macroscopic events, as there surely is, then the indeterminism will infect the macroscopic. For a homely example that suffices to make the point, imagine a physicist deciding that she'll go for lunch after exactly so many clicks of the Geiger counter" (Ladyman, Ross, Spurrett, & Collier, 2010, p. 25).[57]

There is ready evidence for both unpredictable and acausal behavior that demonstrates indeterminacy is part of the design of the universe. If it is admitted that such indeterminacy characterizes the universe, and the clockwork Newtonian model is overthrown, then there remain few barriers to accepting free will. One is the idea that particles carry causality, and then some mechanism need be admitted giving causality to some thing called mind. I have argued that bolts carry causality, not particles. I have argued that mind itself is bolts. Therefore, our common belief is not wrong, and mind itself is a causal agent.

We have been held in the grip of a particle-centric ontology too long, and it obscures obvious facts about how conscious creatures operate in the world. When we jettison this ontological baggage, the replacement causality better explains what we know occurs. Conscious creatures make choices based on a rich web of macro-level observations and meanings in the world and act on these.

As an example: a young woman, a recent college graduate, listens to the radio. She has a mind full of memories, themselves bolts, shaped by parents and friends, ideas passed down in books, and experiences of the world. Perhaps these include the idea of "altruism," and another about "public service." As she listens, she hears the then-President, John F. Kennedy, say, "We choose to go to the Moon! We choose to go ... not because they are easy, but because they are hard." The set of relations that constitutes how the world is at this instant is unique, as is the set of relations that has brought this mind to arrive at this moment. Mentality resolves the relations and the bolts of mind *act*. She resolves to dedicate her life to space exploration.

This is a fully causative mentality, acting with free will, a free will worth having.

Conclusion

I offer a hypothesis about *what there is* by answering that the universe consists entirely of two elements, bolts and booms, really existing within a physically closed universe. I suggest that relations (both bolts and booms) can do the work ascribed to properties and that properties should be retired from the ontological table of elements. Then bolts carry the role of causality, in a closed physical universe, where no objects need exist. The metaphysical handstand redefines long-held ideas about the roles for ontological elements in causation and truth-making. The bolt hypothesis offers a radical new way to conceive of those elements of reality which have existence. It could suggest productive avenues for scientific experimentation. If something like this is at work, then it is more correct to think about the universe as *pattern* rather than as *substance*.

Mental Causation—A Relational Ontology

Here I explore a new perspective on the nature of mind. Motivated by Jaegwon Kim's 1998 discussion, *The Many Problems of Mental Causation*, this response proposes an alternative ontology for mind.

The hypothesis is that mind consists of causal relations. These causal relations, or bolts,[1] are the fundamental causative elements of the universe, rather than objects (or in conventional physics, the particles considered to be the causative elements).

A physicalist, who believes that the universe is real, sees real biological creatures operating in that universe. I propose that, for such creatures, meaning develops out of interaction with their environment. I suggest that from the simplest organisms, conducting processes as simple as digestion, there continues an evolutionary chain to more complex creatures that exhibit various levels of mentality, including sentience and culminating in consciousness. The metaphysical claim about mind is fully consistent with an evolutionary biological description. To illustrate how mind might have evolved in a physical world, I use a biological exemplar and trace its hypothetical development.

The metaphysical claim underpinning this mental ontology is that relations are causative and are patterned in vast webs. To better visualize these webs, I subdivide them into *relational maps*. A *relational map* is defined as a subclass of relation, giving information in an orderly form according to some convention of representation. One map, the lower relational map, consists of the relations among internal states of an organism and its environment. The second, upper relational map, consists of relations among neurons within the physical brain of the organism. Mentality then ontologically is a relation between relations.

I use the intermediate category of *relational maps* to best explain how mentality can develop in the physical world, from simple biological creatures to one embodying our own complex mentality. Recognize that relational maps are just more relations, more bolts, so the claim is that mentality is entirely composed of bolts. Bolts supply an intrinsically centered semantics and give a complete ontological description of mind.

Introduction

What is the nature of mind? The question has bedeviled philosophers for ages. Cartesian dualism distinguished mind from body, preserving the separate soul of Western theologies into modern philosophy. Today, science has found entirely physical explanations for many phenomena, and philosophers embracing a scientific worldview search for a physical solution to the question of mind. Physicalists expect a solution that respects the physical causal closure of the universe. Yet most suggested paths have led to the unsatisfactory positions of emergentism and panpsychism.[2]

Jaegwon Kim offered a forceful statement of the problems of mental causation existent within a physicalist description of mind. His assessment left these problems unresolved and raised the stakes by suggesting that not only causality, but human agency and the possibility of human perception, memory, and human knowledge are at risk. In response to Kim, I suggest that problems of mental causation can be simplified if we embrace a relational ontology of mental events. This ontology preserves a reductionist physicalist mentality without resorting to dualism or metaphysical approaches, which I believe have clouded our understanding of mentality. The overall direction of the argument interweaves (a) the statement of Kim's problems of mental causation, (b) a biological exemplar[3] to promote more grounded analysis, and (c) presentation of a mental ontology that addresses various philosophical constraints and objections, and that answers Kim's main problems of mental causation.

I will use the physical example of a simple organism, *Caenorhabditis elegans (C. elegans)*, to ground the claim in biology and to initiate several thought experiments. The relational ontology provides an answer to Kim's most critical problems of causation. There are implications for related puzzles in the philosophy of mind.

1 Significant Problems of Mental Causation

In his seminal discussion,[4] Kim describes the three most critical problems facing any rational explanation of mental causation. These are (a) the problem of anomalous mental properties, (b) the problem of extrinsic mental properties, and (c) the problem of causal exclusion. Kim describes the first two problems only briefly and focuses most of his attention on the third, most troublesome problem. Kim leaves us boxed in by constraints, with no solution to these problems of mental causation.

Constraints

Kim positions his problems of mental causation within the context of a thoroughgoing physicalism. A key tenet of physicalism[5] is the causal closure of the physical universe, which Kim describes as the principle that "if you pick any physical event and trace out its causal ancestry or posterity, that will never take you outside the physical domain" (Kim, 2002, p. 175). Another strong version of the physical causal closure principle, given by Agustin Vincente, is that "physical effects have *only* physical causes" (2006, p. 150). While not without criticism, some variant of the physical causal closure principle is generally accepted by physicalists, those ascribing to the view that the universe is physical. The primary import of the principle is that it avoids dualist theories of mind, such as Descartes' idea that mental phenomena might be something non-physical.

Kim poses the fundamental question: "How is it possible for the mind to exercise its causal powers in a world that is fundamentally physical?" (2002, p. 171).

Some historical suppositions in the philosophy of mind that Kim implicitly acknowledges constrain solutions to the problems of mental causation. These constraints involve multiple realizability and its minimal manifestation, supervenience. The constraints arose from the debate over identity theories. If whatever is the mental is in some fashion identical with the physical structures of the brain, then it might seem that an easier solution may be found for mental causation within a physically closed universe. But identity theories have been criticized as inadequate. Identity theory says that when we experience something (for example, pain), that experience is exactly reflected by a neurological state. U.T. Place used the analogy of a cloud and a mass of water droplets in suspension to illustrate the identity. Place noted, ". . . that in order to establish the identity of consciousness and certain processes in the brain, it would be necessary to show that the introspective observations reported by the subject can be accounted for in terms of processes that are known to have occurred in his brain" (2002, p. 58). Struggling with the vast gap between molecular processes and the complex psychological behavior exhibited by our minds, Place was quick to say, "I am not claiming that statements about sensations and mental images are reducible to or analyzable into statements about brain processes"[6] (2002, p. 55). As identity theory struggled against behavioral theories of mind, computationalist approaches came to the fore, and the problem became framed in terms of computational mental states.

The examples that Putnam used against identity theory challenged the strong identity between pain and a brain state (Putnam, 1973). He argued that strong identity was species-specific and was a matter of necessity. His examples of 'super Spartans' showed that a behavioral description of pain would fail. Putnam's 'likelihood argument' against brain state (type-identity) theory is that empirical evidence is unlikely to show it to be true, because "if we can find even one psychological predicate which can clearly be applied to both a mammal and an octopus (say 'hungry'), but whose physical-chemical 'correlate' is different in the two cases, the brain-state theory has collapsed" (1973, p. 77). He suggested a requirement for multiple realizability, and this constraint apparently doomed any identity between mental phenomena and the physical substrate.

Multiple realizability permits a single mental kind to be realized by many distinct physical kinds, as illustrated in Diagram 1. Notice that the mental event m might be instantiated by either the physical token p_1 or by p_2 in the physical substrate (which is composed of neurons and biochemicals). We say that m is multiply-realizable. The same mental state can be produced from different physical brain states. For example, one may arguably be in the same state of anxiety upon either hearing one loud clap of thunder (physical substrate in condition p_1) or instead upon hearing two claps of thunder (physical substrate in condition p_2). This leads to a token physicalist interpretation of the interaction between mental events and the underlying physical substrate.

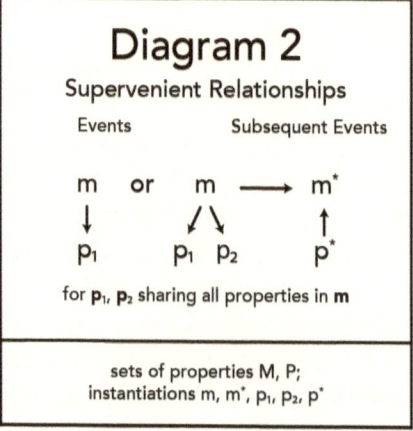

In the philosophy of mind, supervenience has been invoked as a minimal condition for causality that meets the physicalist requirement for closure under the physical universe. Generally, supervenience refers to a relation between sets of properties or sets of facts. The mathematics is: X is said to supervene on Y if and only if some difference in Y is necessary for any difference in X to be possible. Equivalently, X is said to supervene on Y if and only if X cannot vary unless Y varies. When applied to mental causation, supervenience is a set of dependency relationships held between properties of the mind (M) and the physical substrate of the brain (P). Mental properties M are composed of individual mental events (such as m and m* shown in Diagram 2). The base physical properties P are composed of particular physical instantiations of mental events (such as p_1, p_2, and p*). The mental event m may be either singly- or multiply-realizable. The catchphrase for the mental supervenience relationship is, "There cannot be an M-difference without a P-difference." Said more formally, the set of M-properties supervene upon P-properties just in case no two things can differ with respect to M-properties without also differing with respect to their P-properties.

We may use the example (Hare, 1952) (illustrated in Diagram 3) of two pictures hanging on the wall that have some aesthetic, intrinsic difference of goodness. Call the two pictures P and Q. Then, "We cannot say P is exactly like Q in all respects save this one, that P is a good picture and Q is not," for "there must be some *further* difference between them to make one good and the other not" (Hare, 1952, p. 81).

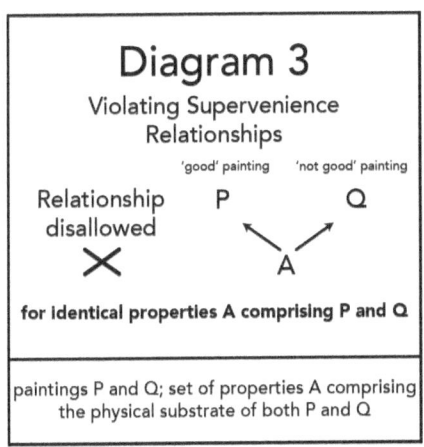

Supervenience constrains the relationship between M and P such that no single configuration of the physical substrate can instantiate two different mental events. Note that the supervenience constraint is not symmetric: it prevents a single physical instantiation from supporting two different mental states, but it does not prevent a mental state or event from being constituted by alternate physical instantiations. Therefore, supervenient mental relationships include those which are multiply-realizable.

If the above supervenience relationships are accepted, then *epiphenomenalism* is an overriding concern. Epiphenomenalism is the philosophical position that argues if mental states are caused by physical states or events, then there is nothing left for mentality to do—the mind causes nothing. Our minds are merely along for the ride.

Kim begins with the physical causal closure principle, then argues that supervenience relationships hold for mental events. Then if mental events are caused entirely by physical events in the brain, he concludes that mentality is an epiphenomenon. In his memorable analogy, Kim says:

> In the case of the supposed M-M* causation, the situation is rather like a series of shadows cast by a moving car; there is no causal connection between the shadow of the car at one instant and its shadow an instant later, each being an effect of the moving car. The moving car represents a genuine causal process, but the series of shadows it casts, however regular and lawlike it may be, does not constitute a causal process. (Kim, 2002, p. 177)

For Kim's problems of mental causation to be solved, mental events must demonstrate true causative power, not be mere shadows of other causes.

Kim's Problems of Mental Causation

Let's sketch the first two of Kim's problems of mental causation, then analyze the third in detail. I will not address the first problem, except to briefly note it, and will circle back later to address the second problem during elaboration on the intrinsic/extrinsic distinction for relations and properties.

The first problem, anomalous mental properties, arises from Davidson's particular claims about psychological phenomena and his proposed solution. Kim summarizes Davidson's monism, that ". . . mental events fall under physical kinds (or have true physical descriptions), from which it follows, argues Davidson, that they are physical events" (Kim, 2002, p. 172). Davidson's claim is followed by his principle, that ". . . there are no strict deterministic laws on the basis of which mental events can be predicted and explained (the Anomalism of the Mental)" (1970, p. 80). The claim is an attempt to preserve free will through the introduction of the mental "anomalism." Many philosophers still consider this to be a problem because it does not answer the question "How can anomalous properties be causal properties?" (Kim, 2002, p. 172).

Kim spends little time addressing this first problem of mental causation. It seems the problem is self-generated by the claim that there are no causal laws about psychological phenomena and of the related claim for an anomalous separation between mental events and physical events. If psychological phenomena do <u>not</u> exist as disconnected causal kinds as proposed by Davidson, this problem of mental causation may be eliminated using Occam's razor. One may admit a robust role for psychology in mentality but deny that it is disconnected. Like Kim, I will not directly address this first problem of mental causation. But I suggest it follows from a relational ontology of mental causation that psychological phenomena need not exist as disconnected kinds, so this first problem of mental causation is not a hurdle.

Second for Kim is the problem of extrinsic mental properties.[7] Kim asks, "How can extrinsic, relational properties be causally efficacious in behavior production?" (2002, p. 173). This problem is motivated by syntacticalism, the doctrine that ". . . only 'syntactic' properties of internal states, not their 'semantic' (or 'content' or 'representational') properties, are psychologically relevant—in particular, to behavior causation" (1993, p. 289). Kim says that semantic properties must be relational and, therefore, extrinsic (2002, p. 173). I agree with Kim that semantics is central (versus syntacticalism's focus on syntax), but following my examination of Kim's fundamental problem of mental causation in Section 3, I will challenge his assertion that a semantic, relational cause is extrinsic.

Third, and most significant, is the problem of causal exclusion. An underlying philosophical idea is that there are nomological lawlike kinds, which lack logical necessity yet, because they resemble general laws, are accepted. In this case, the focus is on mental events as lawlike kinds. There are assumed in this description to be lawlike kinds M and P that follow lawlike nomological rules. Such kinds are composed of individual events (m, p, m*, and p*). In Diagram 4, assume two mental events, one temporally causing the next, with their associated physical instantiations. If we are to believe that our mental states cause temporally related mental states, then m (some prior mental event) must be a cause of m*. We also suppose that mental event m* of mental kind M causes physical event p* of physical kind P. To meet the physical causal closure constraint, physical event p* must have been caused by some prior temporal event p. But since physical event p causes p*, then p* has two causes, both m* and p. We see that p* is over-determined, and there seems to be no real work for mental event m* to do. Kim asks how a mental cause is also possible. I will directly challenge this conundrum with my relational mental ontology.

MENTAL CAUSATION—A RELATIONAL ONTOLOGY

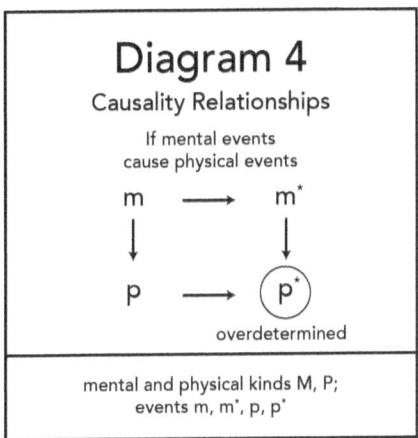

Diagram 4
Causality Relationships
If mental events cause physical events

mental and physical kinds M, P; events m, m*, p, p*

Overdetermination and Epiphenomenalism

Intractable inconsistencies confront any explanation working within the framework of Kim's three problems of mental causation and the constraints imposed by the demands of a physicalist explanation. Kim shows that if mental events and physical events are nomological lawlike kinds, then as a minimal, necessary condition the mental must supervene on the physical (no more robust relationship between M and P, such as some identity relationship, is possible if one accepts Putnam's arguments, which Kim apparently does). Kim says that ". . . if mind-body supervenience fails, there is no visible way of understanding the possibility of mental causation" (2002, p. 175). If one accepts supervenience and accepts the causal closure of the physical universe, then the causal relationships (between m and p, m* and p*) must hold. But the causality relationships resulting from M-P supervenience are not a sufficient condition to avoid epiphenomenalism. Diagram 4 shows that this leads directly to causal overdetermination. Kim suggests no way to avoid the dilemma. What is a physicalist to do? Perhaps Fodor stated best how devastating this result is to everything most philosophers, and people, believe:

> If it isn't literally true that my wanting is causally responsible for my reaching, and my itching is causally responsible for my scratching, and my believing is causally responsible for saying . . ., if none of that is literally true, then practically everything I believe about anything is false and it's the end of the world. (Fodor J. A., p. 156)

This unavoidable result (given the assumptions) does not seem to make any sense given our prevailing understanding of the world, and we need not accept that we have been utterly deceived. I intend to show that the evidence for epiphenomenalism is less obvious and well-grounded than Kim's dilemma suggests, and there is merit in our commonsense view of mental causation. We seem to know that our decision to move our foot leads to our foot moving. It seems that mental events cause physical events. We know that if we stub our toe, we will feel pain in our toe. Physical events cause mental events. If we see a child stub her toe, and if she reacts by crying, we understand that another mind is experiencing a painful experience like one that we have felt in our past. We expect that if we show sympathy to the child, the child can feel our sympathy. Mental events seem to have causal effects relayed via the physical interface of perception, even on other minds. Kim, with most philosophers, would like to account for these intuitions, yet his assessment of the problem suggests they are illusions. The relational ontology intends to support these common explanations of mental causation.

2 Mind as Relationship

Ontological Landscape

To provide a better perspective, let me describe the overall ontological terrain that I will traverse. I suggest that the problem of mental causation is created by a misunderstanding of the ontology of mentality, conflated with ambiguities in the ontology of relations and properties when applied to mentality. We are forced to use *properties* and *natural kinds* in our vocabulary to describe mentality, without understanding what they are. These misunderstandings combine to create the tangled knot of mental causation. I shall proceed by working on one knotty problem, and then on another, to unravel each a bit at a time.

Let's start by accepting realism as ontologically foundational, with a physical world independent of sentient beings. Within the spatiotemporal world, interactions among particles occur in time in groupings which may be called *events*. Given concerns regarding the ontic status of properties, I shall adopt a minimalist stance, avoiding where possible all talk about properties. I will suggest a sparse ontology which respects full closure of the physical domain. Loosely beginning with Kotarbiński's reism[8] (Woleński, 2010), I will borrow his two ontological theses that (a) assume physical objects but (b) allow that no physical object is a state of affairs, relation, or property. The first category in the ontological table is filled with *objects*, which have existence. Second, as soon as we imagine the existence of two objects, then we must necessarily imagine there may be a *relation* between them. Logically, therefore, relation enters into any descriptive ontology whenever the existent universe is more than a monism. Relation must be the second category in the ontological table.

With these sparse ontological commitments, I follow Quine's preference for desert landscapes (Quine W. V., 1948) and assiduously apply Occam's razor to ontological extensions.[9] I shall adhere to a metaphysical nominalism (versus metaphysical realism) for the monadic universals called *prop-*

erties or *kinds*. A property is typically defined as an attribute of an object. The distinction is sometimes made between properties and kinds by saying that objects exhibit *properties* by *possessing* them, and objects demonstrate *kinds* by *belonging to* them. Quine notes "Properties are intensional in that they may be counted as distinct properties even though wholly coinciding in respect of the things that have them. There is no call to reckon kinds as intensional. Kinds can be seen as sets, determined by their members. It is just that not all sets are kinds" (p. 118). To Quine's idea that kinds can be seen as sets, I would elaborate that sets may be seen as relations. Then kinds may be described as a subset of relations, with no need to expand the ontological table.

For many philosophers, a property is considered to be distinct from the objects that possess it, and there is an urge to give properties some ontological reality. I will resist this tendency. Mental events are often described as properties. Such descriptions are used to justify the separate symbol M supervening on a physical substrate P. I delve more deeply into the philosophical discussion of properties in Section 3, but here I suggest that the label *property* is misleading and leads to misunderstanding about the nature of mentality.

Let's define a particular type of relation—a relational map—as a relation giving information in an orderly form according to some convention of representation.

Here are simple examples. We can describe a particular relation between an ant and a drop of water—both real objects, bundles of particles, existing in a real universe—as $R(a, w, i)$, without attributing any additional "essence" or physical existence to that relation. We might identify the relation $R(a, w, 1)$ that the drop of water is "smaller than" the ant, and the relation $R(a, w, 2)$ that the drop of water is "to the right of" the ant in some spatiotemporal coordinate system. As another example, another relational map might consist of the relations among several neurons within an organism, say $R(n_1, n_2, 27)$, a particular relation between the neurons n_1 and n_2. The working definition of a *relational map* gives a more precise starting point, identifying a subclass within the broad term *relation*, before addressing mentality.

Let me now suggest a different way to frame the problem ontologically. Think of mental events exclusively as relations between relational maps. Therefore, ontologically, the mental is a relation between two other relations. *I suggest that the mental is a relation between relational maps.* One relational map consists of the relations among internal states of an organism and its environment. The second relational map consists of relations among neurons or other mental apparatus within the physical brain of the organism. The relation between relational maps supplies an intrinsically centered semantics. *This relation between relational maps is a complete ontological description of the ontology of the mental.* It will require some exposition to tease out the elements of this description, which I will do with analogies, definitions, and a biological exemplar. The relations that describe mentality are contained within a sparse ontology, one which admits only physical objects and relations.[10] This ontology respects the physical causal closure principle.

To support this ontological description of individual mental events, extended temporally to mental activity, I will use the primitive biological organism, *C. elegans*, as a model and exemplar. Using a real organism helps trace through how sensations or perception of the environment, together with internal biological states, result in primitive physical causality. I suggest that this primitive system does exhibit mental activity as very sparsely defined. This biological exemplar serves to initiate a series of thought experiments suggesting an incremental path traversed in evolutionary time by biological creatures on Earth, which might reasonably be seen to lead to more richly inscribed mental activity in higher organisms. There is an enormous mental distance between the sparse mentality of the biological exemplar and conscious beings, and I will not try to address the hard problem of consciousness, nor even the difficult problems linking such sparse mentality to any mentality that approaches consciousness, though the relational ontology does point upward on a path toward that destination.

My argument proposes that the mental activity of simple things like *C. elegans* differs from human mental activity in degree rather than in kind. This proposal is consistent with evolution and the mechanisms of natural selection acting through variation in traits, differential reproduction, and heredity. We might expect mentality to have advanced to a more complex stage in competitive environments where robust mentality would provide an advantage. But to find existing organisms possessing quite a primitive mentality, we must look to protected ecological niches where advanced mentality would confer limited advantages. The soil habitat of *C. elegans* is such a place. By beginning with the simple, I intend to illuminate complex mentality.

A Primitive Biological Exemplar

These thought experiments feature the simple nematode *C. elegans*, which feeds on bacteria such as *Escherichia coli* (*E. coli*). This roundworm is a mere one millimeter long, with a transparent body and a tiny nervous system. Consisting of only 302 neural cells, the nervous system is a cellular network (Brenner, 2002). Summarizing voluminous research, it has been shown to be a small-world network (Watts & Strogatz, 1998), in which there are connected hubs (interneurons), and the mean-shortest path connection can be small. Such networks are very effective designs to interconnect sensory inputs and physical outputs.

C. elegans, a model animal,[11] displays the simplest sensitivity to and perception of its environment. It undulates through its habitat of temperate soils, and one of its central behaviors is, of course, feeding. When the nematode comes across *E. coli*, it senses their presence, and it acts on that perception to ingest the bacteria. When in its dauer larvae stage, *C. elegans* may be transported by invertebrates (such as millipedes and insects).

When it reaches a desirable location, it will get off and feed.

Though it is a primitive organism, the DNA of *C. elegans* contains roughly half of the DNA found in humans.[12] Biology supports the unity of life on Earth and, from the structural similarities,[13] biologists infer that the neural system of *C. elegans* is a simple forerunner of the human neural system. *C. elegans* and *Homo sapiens* also share similarities in biochemical requirements to sustain cellular operation. There is probably an evolutionary path connecting one organism to the other. A physicalist view would likely agree that somewhere on the route between the two organisms, humans (and maybe a few other species) added richly inscribed mental activity and consciousness. Therefore, the proto-mental structure of *C. elegans* may suggest something of the structure of all mentality.

Before using the terms further, let me suggest definitions of mental events and mental activity to be illustrated with examples in *C. elegans*. I use the term *mental event* rather than mental state to highlight its nonstatic, temporal nature. Let me define a mental event as a relation between two relational maps. The first, lower relational map consists of a relation between an entity's environment and its internal physical states. The second, upper relational map consists of a particular arrangement among the neurons (or equivalent apparatus) within the brain of the creature. These can include relations among neurons encoding the entity's memories and beliefs, instantiated at a moment in time. (Memory-forming relations among neurons will be explained more fully with examples. They are assumed to be a later evolutionary improvement and are unnecessary for the basic description.[14]) I will refer to these two relational maps using the shorthand phrases *lower relational map* and upper *relational map*.[15]

A mental event, a relation between two such relational maps, contains semantics (it provides information using signifiers in an orderly form or pattern, imbuing meaning). This definition of mental events encompasses a broad range of activity, resulting in a sparsely defined mentality. The key determinants are that mental events within an organism embody a *relation* between relational maps with that mental relation having inherent *meaning*. One mental event, though, does not instantiate *mental activity*, because clearly there is a longer temporal dimension to mental activity. I will define mental activity by an entity as a series of mental events over a temporal period sufficiently short[16] that the entity can maintain a coherent set of relations and preserve coherent (i.e., meaningful) semantics.

To gain further precision, let's borrow definitions of *perception* and *sensation* from Thomas Reid. Reid said, "The external senses have a double province—to make us feel, and to make us perceive . . . This conception and belief which nature produces by means of the senses, we call *perception*. The feeling which goes along with perception, we call *sensation*" (Reid, 1969). Let's also call the feeling that goes with the status of an internal state a *sensation*.

Returning to the example of feeding *C. elegans*, it seems reasonable to describe the organism as possessing intentionality. The organism feeds when some sensory cue, some sensation, undoubtedly encoded in its neural system, tells it that it needs nutrients (certain biochemicals). When *C. elegans* is no longer hungry (sated with the required nutrients), it stops feeding. If it is hungry and food is not present, the organism may hitch a ride and then get off when it arrives at food. It seems difficult not to describe this observed relationship as displaying intentionality, directed at objects and arrangements of events benefiting the organism in its environment. We observe the obvious actions of *C. elegans* going about its business to survive and multiply. Brentano argued that mental states always have an inherent, intended mental object or content toward which they are directed and, therefore, intentionality is the "mark of the mental" (1955, p. xiii). By Brentano's definition, only mental states exhibit intentionality. These observations suggest that *C. elegans* exhibits at least a sparsely defined mentality.

Definitions of mentality can face issues at both ends of the mentality spectrum. My definition begins at the simplest end and is rooted in biology more than philosophy. Here I point to *C. elegans*. I suggest it is a living biological creature by our everyday definitions—that it exhibits intentionality and that its observed intentionality is more than mechanistic.[17] If mental activity is denied for *C. elegans*, then an alternative explanation must be provided for the observed intentionality. Then a rationale must be given for how and why mental activity is found further up the evolutionary scale.

To those who might argue that *C. elegans* is not sufficiently intentional and, instead, its actions are better described as closer to processes such as digestion, I offer two responses. First, I shall describe several hypothetical examples of how its neurons might be creating representations that should be labeled as mentality. Second, I suggest that if *C. elegans* still doesn't convince, then there is some less-studied organism, slightly further up the evolutionary chain, that serves the same purpose. The argument stands, even without empirical evidence to ground the hypothesis. I have nothing to say to those who deny that life on Earth follows an evolutionary path leading from simplest organisms to our own mentality.

Admittedly this approach is more a definition and an assertion rather than a compelling argument. Let me contrast this approach with the opposite, though, which begins with human consciousness as the exemplar of mentality. There is an inclination then to say about *C. elegans*, "That is not what I meant *at all* when referring to the mental." Philosophical descriptions of human mentality are grounded in semantic distinctions, requiring language as a condition for mentality, and arguably tend toward circularity, as illustrated by the debate regarding intentionality.[18] Granting that the question of a proper definition of mentality is open to serious debate, let me pursue the biological example with a sparse definition of mentality to examine what it may reveal.

We will further explore, with several thought experiments, how this simple creature with only 302 neurons can possess even a sparsely defined mentality. While empirical science will undoubtedly supply a more robust description, I hope here to demonstrate feasibility for a philosophical explanation of mentality that addresses Kim's problems of mental causation.

Syntax and Semantics in Mental Relations

Let's first address whether syntax and semantics exist within the nematode's neural system. Syntax describes the grammatical arrangement of symbols—a set of rules formulating how they may be combined. Semantics suggests there exists meaning embedded within syntactic constructs.

The biological creature *C. elegans* contains a physical substrate of biological tissue with a simple nervous system. Perception or sensory cells interact with its environment, and sensation cells monitor its internal state. Its nervous system forms a relation between perceptual and sensation input and physical output, with a neural network that embodies physical syntax (neural firings), and nascent semantics as *C. elegans* "recognizes" when food is nearby and adapts its behavior (by moving) when nutrients are not available. It seems impossible to deny there is meaning in the nematode's actions, observable in its wise "decisions" that lead to its survival. The crux of intentionality, and of mentality, is semantics (meaning from the organism's viewpoint), and semantics must be a necessary constituent for the intentionality described.

I suggest that semantics is instantiated by dint of the relation between the organism's internal states and its environment. We can imagine that the small-world neural network (encoded by the upper relational map) mirrors relations between sensing cells (sensing the external environment) and cells tracking its internal states (with this relation encoded by the lower relational map) and that this *relation itself* elicits the observed behavior. Such relations constitute a sparsely defined mental activity, but mental activity nonetheless. There is meaning maintained by the instantiation of a series of mental events in a time frame consistent with its environmental dynamics. While bioscience has yet to uncover all its intricacies,

MENTAL CAUSATION—A RELATIONAL ONTOLOGY

we can imagine several levels of biological organization, from neural cells, through biochemical reactions between neurons, down to molecular interactions: a completely closed physical system. For the sparsely defined mental activity of *C. elegans*, each mental event is like the filling inside an Oreo cookie which synchronizes the two relational maps.

What is going on in these mental events, making up this "little mind" of *C. elegans*?[19] We might imagine a primitive semantics (which I portray using an invented notation[20]) that consists of such states as "need food" (internal sensing state N), "food sensed" (external perceptual state F), "move to food" (locomotion action L), "eat food" (ingestion action E), and "move around" (general locomotion action G). The nematode holds in its little mind the relationship {N&~F→G}. Or, it may think {N&F →L&E} when it has identified and eats food. The payoff for this "little thought" at the biochemical level is that biochemicals are delivered to the organism. The "little thought" {N&F→L&E} therefore is also describable as a closed biochemical loop, and as a relation that links the organism with its environment. When certain of these states are connected, neurochemical and biochemical reactions are initiated. A feedback loop is started that may be self-organizing.[21] All these relations between the organism (and its states) and the environment are synchronized with the second set of relations, connections among the 302 neural cells in the roundworm, that is, entirely physically.

To enlarge my Oreo cookie analogy, we might imagine that each of the above statements constitutes a cookie. Each lower side of the cookie relates the internal/external state of the organism, which is related to its internal neural machinery on the upper side of the cookie. The nematode's mental activity consists of a line of cookies, with the semantics of each faintly distinguishable. With its limited semantic vocabulary, the organism can make only elementary distinctions. The neural network fires to instantiate another cookie and the nematode engages in meaningful action. The relation instantiated in each cookie broadly spans from sensation or perception of the external world to internal states and sensations.[22] These elementary cookies earn immediate benefits for the organism. For the nematode, it's "all about me." This ontology for mental events instantiates a juvenile intentional agency by its very nature. The feedback relation between the organism and its environment likely created the convention of representation that became encoded in the neural network. Primitive semantics probably came about in this fashion, bootstrapped from the relation.

As much as this explanation seeks simplicity, admittedly it is complex in its details, with sets of relations constituting both the lower and upper relational maps. The need for nutrients (N) is evidenced in multiple cells. The sensing of food on the membrane of *C. elegans* occurs at multiple cells. Similarly, the upper relational map is made up of multiple relations among neurons. Just the simple mental event {N&F} is a relation between sets of relations. One mental event evidences the relation between the organism and its environment at one precise moment in time. Neurons fire, and in the next moment the neural state is changed. The world has also changed. The next mental event depends again on the new lower and upper relational maps at that instant. The result is intentional, not merely mechanistic (like digestion) because the organism's behavior can be specified by relational bodily movements. This distinction was made by Bermúdez (2003, p. 195).

That does not answer for the necessary and sufficient characteristics for mentality. Those specified by the earlier definition of mental activity are minimal necessary characteristics. Likely some membrane to separate "inside" from "outside" is also necessary to preserve coherent relations. A membrane allows the relation to remain intrinsically centered on the organism (i.e., then there is an entity around which the relation is centered in space). Sufficiency conditions might be met when two things happen: (a) connections (via mechanisms such as biochemical feedback loops) repeat under the same conditions, and (b) a repertoire of connections is available that repeat under varying environmental conditions. For example, an organism may minimally need both the relation {N&F→L&E} and the relation {N&~F→G}. These necessary and sufficient characteristics do not preclude mental activity in non-biological entities (so electronically based entities might develop mental activity, especially if creatures such as us serviceably arrange conditions). But given the chemical nature of the universe, it is not likely that unaided mental activity develops this way.

    A result of this description is that mechanistic biochemical reactions came first, followed by semantics (with simple signifiers consisting of the internal/external relation), and later followed by syntax.[23] The first semantics were found in a simple neural (or initially biochemical) connection that allowed a biochemical reaction. Just as turning on an electrical switch causes electrons to flow (and can then cause a light bulb to light up), so the neural connection causes biochemicals to flow.[24] Those connections that worked for the organism were conserved by evolution. The semantic meaning of "supplying biochemical nutrients" (or "assuaging hunger") was an *a posteriori* conceptual meaning growing out of a biochemical fact. The syntactical (symbolic) structures and "set of rules" of syntax to represent more robust concepts such as "hunger" then developed after the primitive semantics. While conjectural, this provides a consistent evolutionary account of how semantics might have become instantiated by simple biochemical connections sorted through an evolutionary "Sieve of Eratosthenes,"[25] with countless[26] useless connections removed.

    This evolutionary account for mentality suggests that semantics came early in its development before complex syntax came about. The thesis is that the order of development was (a) simple biochemical connections, followed by (b) meaning growing out of logical sets of such connections that preserved repeating processes, developing into (c) more elaborate sets of processes that together constituted a nascent intentionality, with (d) the neural network then encoding syntax. The ordering offers advantages compared to syntacticalism, with its focus on syntax over semantics, about the riddle of how meaning can be grounded. Kim notes that "Syntacticalism most naturally arises in the context of computationalism, an approach that urges us to view mental processes as computational processes on internal representations, on the model of information processing in digital computers" (2002, p. 173). Computational theories of mind (CTM) assert that mental processes are performed in ways responsive to the syntax of symbolic representations. Such models of mentality, however, fail to supply adequate semantic meaning. My claim is that CTM have evolutionary history backward. I think that semantics developed first from simple biochemical connections, and these connections provided grounding for meaning. The organism is reliably connected to its environment, and organisms with any breakdown in the connection would not survive. This is a solution to the "symbol grounding problem"—how semantic interpretation of a formal symbol system can be made intrinsic to the system—that stymies computationalist theories of mind (Harnad, 1990). I think representations developed later in evolutionary time allowed richly inscribed mentality. By beginning with a simple biological exemplar instead of human mentality, the attractiveness of this evolutionary ordering becomes more obvious.

Computers employ computer software that encodes only syntax. When I look at a button on the screen of my cell phone, that button is instantiated in software with a particular syntax. None of the semantics exist in the cell phone that let me know what the button does, or even that there is an object that might be called a button. The semantics exist in the relationship between me and the device, and my mind with its intentionality adds that meaning. By the relational definition of mentality, neither the digital computer nor the cell phone contains mental events, because neither completely instantiate the relation constituting semantic meaning. The analogy to computers misdirects our attention from systems that embody both syntax and semantics (such as biological systems) to ones that embody only syntax and overlooks that the human creators or users of the computer program provide the semantics. The relational mental ontology supports Kim's arguments against the syntactic theory of mind (in which semantics plays no explanatory role),[27] as it suggests a central role for semantics and only a supporting role for syntax.

The Role of Memory

In the relational ontology, the relation that is mind must constantly synchronize between the lower relational map and the upper relational map found in the neurons. The lower relational map (the ontological description) between organism and environment (the physical description) acts as an anchor to reality, with all its temporal dynamics. The upper relational map (the ontological description) is a web of relations among connected neurons (the physical description). For the simplest imaginable organisms, my guess is that the neuronal network must transfer signals that maintain sufficient synchronization, instantiating the entire relation bridging from internal states and motor control neurons to sensors of the external environment. The relation on the upper relational map mirrors the relation on the lower relational map. Otherwise, the organism isn't tracking the relation between itself and its environment, and mentality (and meaning to the organism, and intentionality) collapses.

But what of memory? Kim says that "If you take away perception, memory, and reasoning, you pretty much take away all of human knowledge" (2002, p. 171). I'll now fortify the relational ontology with an account of memory to fill out the definition of a mental event by introducing a second thought experiment using our nematode. The thought experiment shows there is no philosophical reason that memories could not have developed from relations that operated both biochemically and neurally. The hypothetical example is supported by empirical evidence that biological systems work in a similar manner.

Without memory, every organism necessarily must instantiate the particular relation that constitutes a particular meaning at that moment. But it would be more efficient if, after practicing these relations (to initially instantiate meaning), the organism could somehow shortcut the process. If only a portion of the instantiated relation might recreate the whole, then less effort would be needed. For example, we might ask how the relation {N&~F→G} might be instantiated at the level of individual neurons by the relation {n_1&~f_1→g_1}. Alternatively, there may be several neurons sensing lack of food (~f_1, ~f_2). Then maybe some interneuron might form a synaptic connection to "stand in" for the relation of these, temporally adjusting the relation and saving energy. In that case, the sensing neurons (~f_1&~f_2) would be connected to the gateway interneuron h_1. When it fired, the relation {n_1&~h_1→g_1} would be equivalent to the relation {n_1&(~f_1&~f_2) →g_1}. This doesn't suggest that the neurons (~f_1&~f_2) would cease firing, but rather that the interposition of the gateway neuron h_1 could make firing more temporally efficient. So even if the timing of the base level neurons (~f_1&~f_2) were episodic, the gateway neuron h_1 would keep track of that relational subpart and could thereby instantiate the balance of the relation in a shorter spatiotemporal span. I suggest that such a gateway neuron h_1 is a memory. Memory eliminates the need for the complete relation to be instantiated again, but instead, a neural (and biochemical) instantiation serves the same purpose for a subset of the relation.[28] Evolution would allow the substitution, so long as the relation supplemented by memory instantiated a similar meaning that was useful. The meaning of the original instantiation must be accessible as part of the relation, setting a minimal threshold for the biochemical state that is the memory.

The second thought experiment is hypothetical, but the actual "wiring" among neurons is an empirical question. While

MENTAL CAUSATION—A RELATIONAL ONTOLOGY

mapping of the neural network of *C. elegans* is incomplete, results already support its reality in biology. This research shows there are sensory neurons dedicated to sensory perception and these are connected to interneurons in the manner described (Oshio, et al., 2003). Philosophy must await science for a complete description of the mechanism but, clearly, memory can be described physically, supporting this ontological description of the upper relational map.

I said earlier that the relational mental ontology eliminates *exclusive* dependence on symbols or representations. It doesn't suggest that symbols or representations do not exist at all; on the contrary, I think they exist physically in the brain through the mechanisms described, both nonconceptually and conceptually. The second thought experiment plausibly explains how memory evolved in biology, and how memories might be instantiated at the biochemical and neural levels. It suggests that organisms "boot up" the semantics from broad relations between the organism and the environment, and then memories are neural (and biochemical) instantiations of parts of the relationships sufficient to complete meaning.[29]

I have used the example of *C. elegans* to show how a sparsely defined mentality can have developed in a real creature. The thought experiments show that semantics could have developed from relations that are formed between the creature and its environment, through evolutionary processes operating through countless trials. These relations supply intrinsically centered semantics. Meaning itself is bootstrapped from processes that in origin nearly resemble non-mental biochemical activity, such as digestion. I argue that *C. elegans* exemplifies a creature exhibiting intentionality and, therefore, at least a sparsely defined mentality. With only 302 neurons, *C. elegans* has crossed the chasm to some mentality. Philosophers must leave the burden to empirical science to describe the details of this crossing. We need to note that intentionality is exhibited, that it is possible to provide a purely physical explanation for such intentionality, that such intentionality must characterize at least a sparsely defined mentality, and that it exists in very simple creatures such as *C. elegans*. I will now return to Kim's main problems of mental causation.

3 Kim's Main Problems of Mental Causation Answered

A Response to the Problem of Causal Exclusion

Kim's central problem of mental causation is the problem of physical causal exclusion. We look to describe mentality within a physical universe, avoiding appeals to some non-physical hand-waving. We look to an explanation consistent with science. Kim asks, "Given that every physical event that has a cause has a physical cause, how is a mental cause also possible?" (2002, p. 174). The relational ontology provides an answer.

To put a point on this ontological claim, let me highlight again how a mental event is a relation between two relational maps, both of which are themselves relations among physical entities. One is a relational map formed by dint of the entity's relation with its environment, that is, a relation between physical objects (such as the particular relation between an ant and a drop of water, $R(a, w, 1)$). The second relational map is of a relation among neurons, say $\{n_1, n_2\}$ between the neurons n_1 and n_2. This relational map is also a relation between physical material, formed of biochemicals in the physical substrate, and, at lower levels of description, particles in motion. The mental event is the relation between the two relational maps. Sequences of mental events, sequences of relations, constitute mental activity. So M and P do not denote different kinds, and there is no need to invoke properties p, p*; individual instantiating signifiers of m, m*, {n}, {n*}, (oe) and (o-e)* are merely to help with bookkeeping. The "parts of a cookie" serve as a bridge metaphor to previous use in philosophical literature, but we should be focused on the whole cookie. When one cookie follows another cookie, the row of cookies constitutes causal mental activity. Mental activity is not epiphenomenal because of its ontology.

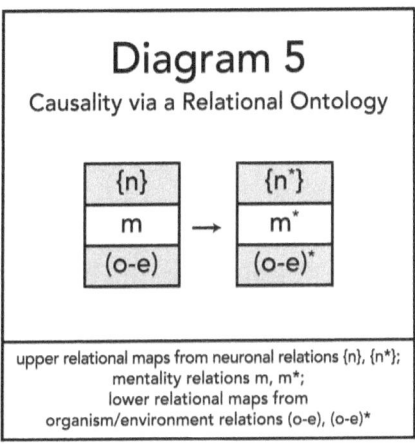

Diagram 5
Causality via a Relational Ontology

upper relational maps from neuronal relations {n}, {n*};
mentality relations m, m*;
lower relational maps from
organism/environment relations (o-e), (o-e)*

Let's use one more example from further up the evolutionary ladder. Imagine the mental event in the interaction between an ant and a drop of water. The ant experiences internal, cellular sensory signals indicating a lack of water and perceives the presence of water in its immediate environment. The relation between the ant and its environment is represented by R(a, w, 2). This relationship between the organism and its environment prompts a similar biochemical connection among neurons within the ant's brain. In the example, neurons in the ant's brain connect internal monitoring of cellular needs $\{n_1\}$ and perception of the presence of water $\{w_1\}$ with locomotion directed toward the water $\{l_1\}$ and activation of muscles for drinking the water $\{d_1\}$, encoding the neuronal inspired relation $\{n_1 \& w_1 \rightarrow l_1 \& d_1\}$. Metaphysically, the two sets of physical processes create relations. Mentality is the relation between these relations. In the example, the mental relations $\{N\&W \rightarrow L\&D\}$ constitute the mental events. Such an interaction (between the ant and drop of water) would, of course, be constituted of many mental relations. But the metaphysical description would remain simple, composed only of relations. The metaphysical description has no need for properties, or for any hierarchical differences between the metaphysical components.

For philosophers, *natural kind* is a grouping of things which has in common something which distinguishes it from other things, and this difference is natural (stemming from the natural world).[30] Scientific disciplines, particularly the biosciences, have flexible references to kinds. For example, viruses mutate, and biosciences have difficulty specifying conditions for kind membership. Philosophical kinds do not mutate as often. Descartes made a point of distinguishing the mental "substance" from the physical substance of atoms in motion, and philosophy has not shaken off the urge to classify the mental and physical as separate natural kinds. Here I intend to question the reoccurrence of this Cartesian tendency. For example, returning to Kim's analogy of the moving car and the shadows representing mental kinds, we find the same error. Mental events should not be considered merely the shadows but part of the car itself. There is no epiphenomenalism because mental events are fully physically causative of the organism's intentional actions.

One problem with using the terminology of properties and natural kinds is that it implies a mathematical inviolability to the physical and mental components under examination. Remember that to answer Kim, we need to find a fully physical solution to the nature of mind. Here is offered a clear ontological description (a relation), built on fully physical elements. The physical structures, which both the lower and upper relational maps are relating, imbue the mental relation with more flexibility (flexibility in semantic meaning) than the inviolable 'natural kinds' of mental properties might suggest. This approach concedes that meaning can be sometimes ambiguous, less than an ideal natural kind. Any mentality is a continuous effort by the organism to maintain the coherence of semantic content, to bridge between its internal needs and desires and the external world.

Supervenience, Multiple Realizability, and Token Physicalism

The relational ontology offers a response to Kim that avoids epiphenomenalism. I need to still address the related constraints of supervenience and multiple realizability. These concepts entered the philosophical discussion as "solutions" to earlier difficulties, as token physicalism replaced identity theory. These theories led away from the ontology advanced here. An example using the biological exemplar can sort through these constraints in a consistent manner. My contention is that multiple realizability and supervenience are secondary issues, grown from a fixation on classifying the mind and the physical as separate natural kinds. In a relational ontology of mind, relational maps may be sufficiently synchronized so natural kinds in the description are superfluous, and associated concerns about the particular wiring become secondary.

Let's initiate a third thought experiment with our nematode about how mental events might be instantiated at the cellular level. Imagine that we wish to describe how *C. elegans* instantiates the thought that it needs food, senses no food nearby, and needs to move around to locate food. The relation was described as $\{N\&\sim F \rightarrow G\}$. The example of memory suggested that the neural instantiation might be either $\{n_1 \& \sim f_1 \rightarrow g_1\}$ or $\{n_1 \& (\sim f_1 \& \sim f_2) \rightarrow g_1\}$. That is, internal sensing of hunger together with either (a) single or (b) multiple perceptual cell firing signaling lack of food in the vicinity may instantiate in our nematode very similar mental states that cause movement. If one provisionally accepts the stipulation that these are very similar mental states, then this is an example of multiple realizability.

We can correspondingly imagine instantiation in a form to fit the definitions of token physicalism. We might imagine a gradient of hunger, from, for example, $\{n_1\}$, $\{n_1 \& n_2\}$, $\{n_1 \& n_2 \& n_3\}$, etc. The last might be instantiated as $\{(n_1 \& n_2 \& n_3) \& {\sim} f_1 \to (g_1 \& g_2)\}$. Here, our nematode exerts more effort moving about (time is pressing). As the feeling of hunger can have degrees, so can impetus to action. The preceding examples are all variations on the general mental relation $\{N \& {\sim} F \to G\}$ and they follow supervenience rules. We might interpret these cases as different degrees of "anxiety" within our nematode, brought about by increasing hunger.[31]

For *C. elegans*, we may carve up the instantiated neural relations into classes and focus on those associated with a particular semantic meaning that we wish to study—anxiety, for example. The question of which neural relations instantiate a particular generalized mental state (e.g., anxiety)—that is, the definition of what classes have meaning—will be determined empirically by the organism operating in its environment. It seems reasonable to suppose that the nematode has no evolutionary need for fifty different mental versions of anxiety, even if it had fifty sensory neurons generally devoted to sensing its environment. Perhaps the sensory input would be summarized by a connecting intermediate neuron, with that interneuron keeping track of an environmentally suitable level of information. So $\{n_1\}$ or $\{n_1 \& n_2\}$ may be summarized in the interneuron h_2. We observe the mental relation $\{h_2 \& {\sim} f_1 \to g_1\}$, and the nematode "feels" some gradation of anxiety. In this hypothetical example, the neuronal substrate may contain multiply-realizable instantiations of anxiety.

From this digression into hypothetical details, we come to the main point. The meaning of "anxiety" found in these example neural relations is instantiated by the entire relation. The ontology of the meaning is likewise the entire mental relation. At first blush, the preceding discussion about multiple realizability and token physicalism used the terms in a manner similar to that employed by philosophers of mind. On closer inspection, however, we can see this is not true. The standard reading of multiple realizability and token physicalism assumes that there are different natural kinds, justifying the separate symbols M and P. Yet here, I only used symbols (N, F, and G) to describe the components of semantic content and to give hypothetical biomechanical examples of how individual neurons (n_1, n_2, h_2, f_1, g_1) might complete the semantic relation that instantiates the meaning "anxiety." If meaning is an outcome of the relational instantiation, we can offer a simpler explanation than posed by the standard philosophical description employing multiple realizability, token physicalism, and supervenience. Difficult as it is to describe such simple mental events as anxiety within the 302 neurons of *C. elegans*, we shudder at trying to do so within the network of roughly 100 billion neurons in the typical human brain. But once we accept the relational ontology of mind, these subjects become merely subsidiary questions of physical wiring.

The ontology allowing that the mental and physical are different kinds, and therefore deserve separate symbols M and P, clouds our understanding of what is going on. In contrast, the relational ontology provides a satisfactory and simpler explanation. The above example of multiple realizability is a case in point. If similar relations instantiate the same action g_1 (in the relation $\{n_1 \& {\sim} f_1 \to g_1\}$, or the relation $\{(n_1 \& n_2) \& {\sim} f_1 \to g_1\}$, or the relation $\{h_2 \& {\sim} f_1 \to g_1\}$, then there could be found a multiple realizability resulting in similar semantic meaning.[32] That is why I can describe these as very similar mental states. The relational mental ontology describes a structure that allows for flexibility in the attribution of meaning while synchronizing the lower and upper relational maps in a correspondence. We really want to know how the light bulb goes off in our brain when we have a thought or feeling. As a bad light bulb joke, we might ask, "How many neurons does it take to screw in a light bulb (i.e., to instantiate a mental event)?" Answer: As many as needed to bridge a coherent relation. How many is that? Ask evolution.

The relational mental ontology allows for flexibility between the lower relational map and the upper relational map, and this flexibility avoids the challenges posed by Putnam and others. Flexibility arises for four reasons. The lower relational map is flexible because there are unlimited ways that the organism can relate to its environment, as the previous example with *C. elegans* illustrates. Second, the neural machinery of a creature might instantiate a corresponding upper relational map in various ways. We can imagine quality differences in constructing both lower and upper relational maps. Third, the relationship between the relational maps is flexible. We can imagine that the quality of thoughts produced depends on all three relationships (using as a measure of quality the fidelity between the mental relation and its correspondence to the external world). Richer, higher-quality relational maps lead to greater precision, fidelity, and depth of thoughts. Fourth, grounding of meaning in the lower relational map is flexible. I submit that grounding of meaning in the lower relational map is *a posteriori* in evolutionary time to the original biochemical instantiation. How this meaning developed richness was somewhat a matter of chance, but the thesis is that evolutionary pressures nurtured meaning. The biological exemplar helps us imagine how the links between the relations comprising mentality may have developed. The example suggests flexibility among the relations, providing sufficient correspondence between the relational maps comprising mentality to provide meaning. From the example for *C. elegans*, we can imagine multiple ways that "anxiety" might be instantiated, and that (more or less) the same meaning can be imagined to be found in both a mammal and an octopus, employing different instantiations. Avoiding the machinery of natural kinds to precisely define anxiety, the relational ontology describes a practical link between the physical and the mental that results in meaning.

Extrinsic Mental Properties

Within Kim's three problems of mental causation, there remains one concern found in his second problem, the problem of extrinsic mental properties. To secure the relational ontology, I argue that mentality need not be described as an extrinsic relation; mentality can be described as an intrinsic relation and be causative.

The relational ontology of mental events challenges two claims that Kim makes about 'extrinsic mental properties.' First, Kim says that "semantic properties of internal states are not in general supervenient on their *synchronous internal* properties, for as a rule they involve facts about the organism's history and ecological conditions" (2002, p. 173). The relational ontology removes any need for this supervenience (i.e., supervenience on synchronous internal properties) because we need not invoke properties or the separate natural kinds that have been conflated with property talk. Second, Kim admits that semantic properties are relational, but he denies that such relational properties could be the basis of mental states. Kim says, ". . . that a given intentional state of an organism instantiates a certain semantic property is a relational fact, a fact that essentially involves the organism's relationship to various external environmental and historical factors" (2002, p. 173). I agree. Kim then says that "[t]his makes semantic properties relational, or extrinsic, whereas we expect causative properties involved in behavior production to be nonrelational, or intrinsic, properties of the organism" (2002, p. 173). The relational ontology differs from Kim on this point. Since mentality is a relation between the lower and upper relational maps, the semantic relations are *intrinsic to that relation*. The relation between relational maps supplies intrinsically centered causative semantics. The response to Kim's second problem of mental causality is that causative semantics embodied in the mental relationship, which itself is a relationship between two relational maps, both mapping to physical things, with both relational maps following the organism while it moves in physical space. This physical fact obviates Kim's main objection and prime reason for expecting a strictly intrinsic property. Therefore, I do not find sufficient grounds for his contention that causative properties must be nonrelational and intrinsic.

Here, a counterexample may summarize how a relation can be causative: If I touch a live electrical wire with the back of my hand, there are two effects: it causes the muscles in my fingers to contract (a relation moving an organic entity within its environment), and it causes pain (the relation embodied in my neuronal substrate). The relation is intrinsic in the most relevant manner.

The distinction between intrinsicality and extrinsicality is bound up in the debate between properties and relations, so both subjects must be addressed to discover an appropriate classification for mental relations. The intrinsic-versus-extrinsic classification gains importance for properties when taken with the claim that extrinsic properties cannot be causative. That is, an objection to causation can be made when talking about objects with purely extrinsic properties: how can purely external properties, independent of an object, have causative powers? But this argument falters against the present ontology, in which mental events are relations (not properties), and so causative power is not purely external.

There is also much debate about the precise definitions of intrinsic and extrinsic, particularly as applied to relations. Philosophers have typically distinguished between something that is intrinsic versus something extrinsic in three ways: (a) relational-versus-nonrelational properties, (b) qualitative-versus-nonqualitative properties, and (c) interior-versus-exterior properties. The relational-versus-nonrelational distinction does not always apply. If we use the example of *having longer legs than arms*, which is a relationship applied to an object—a person—since these are intrinsic to that person (a person defined to include her entire body), then simply being a relation does not entail that the property is extrinsic. The second, qualitative-versus-nonqualitative distinction suggests that any property for which duplicates never differ is intrinsic. Kim introduced the property of *loneliness* as belonging to something that does not coexist with any contingent object wholly distinct from itself (Kim, 1982). The opposite property is *accompanied*. Kim's idea is that intrinsic properties are those properties compatible with loneliness, whereas extrinsic properties, on the contrary, imply accompaniment. Lewis objected that *loneliness* itself is a property that could belong to something lonely, and would, therefore, be an extrinsic property, though obviously not a relational property (Langton & Lewis, 1988). Suffice it to say the qualitative-versus-nonqualitative distinction has not gained full support, and it is less clear how it might apply to relations. The third distinction typically used is the interior-versus-exterior distinction. Given this distinction as the relevant one, intrinsic is defined as a property that an object has by virtue of itself, depending on no other thing. By this definition, a mental event could be classified either way, since it is a relation between relational maps. In the relational description of mentality, the lower relational map appears to be extrinsic (composed of parts both intrinsic and extrinsic). The upper relational map consists of relations among neurons or other mental apparatus within the physical brains of creatures, which is intrinsic. Therefore, the third standard distinction also leads to ambiguity.

If we look to commentators focusing on relations, then the applicable intrinsic/extrinsic label becomes clearer. Clementz (2007) notes,

> However, *intrinsic* and *extrinsic* clearly have further connotations, more *en rapport* with their etymology, that the standard definition given above does not fully capture. As traditional philosophers would have understood it, the phrase 'intrinsic property' conveys the idea (or the metaphor) of a property pertaining, some way or other, to the inherent nature of its bearer. An 'extrinsic property,' by contrast, would be one

that remains purely external—and, as it were, somewhat foreign—to the very nature of the things by which it is instantiated. (2007, p. 170).

By this reading of Clementz, mental events as relations would be intrinsic because the nature of mentality, carried around with an organism, surely is inherent to the nature of its bearer. Clementz develops further distinctions, introducing his concept of *directly constitutive* relations, in which the relation is essential to at least one of the *relata*. He says,

> Armed with these distinctions, we can now return to the question with which we began: are all relational properties *extrinsic* properties in the narrow, more demanding (though, admittedly, somewhat metaphorical) sense of that word? At the first blush, it would seem that relational properties generated by purely external relations are, indeed, extrinsic in *this* sense. By the same token, those which are associated with *strongly* internal—and, above all, with *directly constitutive*—relations should be counted, on the contrary, as intrinsic: indeed, the latter are cases of what T. L. S. Sprigge (1988) calls *intrinsic connectedness*. (Clementz, 2007, p. 177)

From this assessment, mental events as relations are directly constitutive—essential to the *relata* of the internal neuronal structure—and therefore intrinsic.

The various distinctions do not completely account for relations as intrinsic or extrinsic, but lean toward an intrinsic characterization for mental relations. Arguing for intrinsic mental relations, we find (a) the interior-versus-exterior distinction (as partially supportive), (b) the characterization of mentality as inherent to the nature of its bearer, and (c) that mental relations are directly constitutive. On balance, it seems that Kim overreaches by claiming that semantic, relational properties must be extrinsic for mental events. My claim that mental events are intrinsically centered focuses on the salient fact that the mental relation is spatiotemporally centered on the organism. Mental events can be relations between relational maps, with mentality both causative and intrinsic.

Conclusion

We began with seemingly intractable problems of mental causation posited by Kim and, in particular, the main problem of describing mental causation without embracing epiphenomenalism. Adhering to Kim's constraint regarding physical causal closure, I propose a relational ontology of mind as a solution. I claim that mentality is a relation between relational maps, where the relational maps are themselves relations. Mentality relates the relational map of the neuronal machinery to the relational map relating the organism and its environment, with that mental relation supplying the semantics.

The argument is consolidated using a biological exemplar to help ground it in real biology. Since intentionality has been linked so closely to mentality, we should explain the intentionality exhibited by the teeming profusion of life that surrounds us. I propose that simple biochemical reactions lead to semantics, at first trivially, and meaning itself develops as the organism bumps into its environment. The thought experiments with *C. elegans* suggest how meaning is inscribed onto the world by our mental relations. They show how semantics can have developed first, with syntax following later in evolutionary time. Supervenience and multiple realizability become secondary questions of physical wiring, and we can abandon the Cartesian duality between the different 'kinds' of mind and body.

The relational ontology provides a consistent physicalist solution to Kim's main problems of mental causation. With mind as a relation between relations, overdetermination is avoided because the mental and physical are tightly synchronized. The description avoids Kim's main objections against extrinsic relational 'properties' and shows how the mental relation can be both causative and intrinsic.

Elsewhere[38] I suggest that relations—bolts—are the fundamental causative element in the universe. If this hypothesis is true, then causative bolts describe the two relational maps and the relations that link them; all are simply causative bolts. This is the simple path to claim that our minds are causal, and they are not epiphenomena.

The claim of a relational mental ontology has surprisingly broad implications. It answers Kim's main problems of mental causation. It provides a possible answer to what is the mind itself. The relational mental ontology avoids epiphenomenalism, non-reductionism, dualism, emergentism, and panpsychism. The metaphysical hypothesis together with the example of *C. elegans* illustrates how such an explanation can be fully consistent with one from evolutionary biology. These insights come about by examining the beginning of life, to ask how primitive intentionality might advance mentality—a fully causative mentality—in a physical world.

References

Alley, C. (1981). Proper Time Experiments in Gravitational Fields with Atomic Clocks, Aircraft, and Laser Light Pulses. In P. Meystre, & M. O. Scully (Ed.), Quantum Optics, Experimental Gravity, and Measurement Theory (pp. 363-427). Plenum Press.

Aristotle. (1984). The Complete Works of Aristotle, Prior Analytics (Vol. One). (J. Barnes, Ed.) Princeton, NJ: Princeton University Press.

Aspect, A., Dalibard, J., & Roger, G. (1982, December). Experimental Test of Bell's Inequalities Using Time-Varying Analyzers. Physical Review Letters, 49(25), 1804-1807.

Bell, J. S. (1964). On the Einstein Podolsky Rosen Paradox. Physics, 195-200.

Bermúdez, J. L. (2003). Nonconceptual Content: From Perceptual Experience to Subpersonal Computational States. In Y. H. Gunther (Ed.), Essays on Nonconceptual Content (pp. 183-216). Cambridge, MA: MIT Press.

Blaxter, M. (n.d.). Introduction to Caenorhabditis elegans. Retrieved from Caenorhabditis elegans WWW Server: http://www.nematodes.org/Caenorhabditis/index.shtml

Block, N. (2002). Troubles With Functionalism. In D. Chalmers (Ed.), Philosophy of Mind, Classical and Contemporary Readings (pp. 96-97). New York: Oxford University Press.

Bradley, F. (1893). Appearance and Reality: A Metaphysical Essay. New York: Swan Sonnenschein & Co.

Brenner, S. (2002, December 8). Nature's Gift To Science. Retrieved 2010, from Nobel Prize; Nobel Lectures: http://nobelprize.org/nobel_prizes/medicine/laureates/2002/brenner-lecture.pdf

Brentano, F. (1955). Psychology from an Empirical Standpoint. New York: Routledge.

Broad, C. D. (1923). Scientific Thought. London: Routledge & Kegan Paul.

Butterfield, J. (1984). Seeing the Present. Mind, 93, 161-76.

Callender, C. (2008). The Common Now. Philosophical Issues, A Supplement to Nous; Volume 18, Issue 1, 339-361.

Chalmers, D. J. (2002). Consciousness and Its Place in Nature. In D. Chalmers (Ed.), Philosophy of Mind: Classical and Contemporary Readings (pp. 247-272). New York: Oxford University Press.

Clauser, J. F., & Horne, M. A. (1974). Experimental Consequences of Objective Local Theories. Physical Review D, 10(2), 36, 1223-1226.

Clementz, F. (2007). Relational Truthmakers. In J.-M. Monnoyer (Ed.), Metaphysics and Truthmakers (pp. 163-198). New Jersey: Transaction Books.

Compton, A. H. (1931). The Uncertainty Principle and Free Will. Science, 74(1911), 172.

Davidson, D. (1970). Mental Events. In L. Foster, & J. W. Swanson (Eds.), From Experience and Theory (pp. 79-101). Amherst: University of Massachusetts Press.

Dennett, D. C. (2007). "Could Have Done Otherwise" (extract from Elbow Room). In H. Beebee, & J. Dodd, Reading Metaphysics: Selected Texts with Interactive Commentary (pp. 82-99). Maiden, MA: Blackwell Publishing.

Dennett, D. C. (2002). Quining Qualia. In Philosophy of Mind, Classical and Contemporary Readings (pp. 226-246). New York: Oxford University Press.

Eddington, A. S. (1932). The Decline of Determinism. Presidential Address to the Mathematical Association, 1932. The Mathematical Gazette, 16(218), 66-80.

REFERENCES

Einstein, A., Poldolsky, B., & Rosen, N. (1935). Can Quantum-Mechanical Description of Physical Reality Be Considered Complete? Physical Review, 47(10), 777.

Eisberg, R., & Resnick, R. (1985). Quantum Physics of Atoms, Molecules, Solids, Nuclei, and Particles (Second Edition ed.). USA: John Wiley& Sons, Inc.

Finkelstein, D. (1958). Past-Future Asymmetry of the Gravitational Field of a Point Particle. Physical Review, 110(4), 965-967.

Fodor, J. (1988). Psychosemantics: The Problem of Meaning in the Philosophy of Mind. Cambridge, MA: MIT Press.

Fodor, J. A. (1990). Chapter 5: Making Mind Matter More. In A Theory of Content and Other Essays. Cambridge, MA: MIT Press.

Giustina, M., Mech, A., Ramelow, S., Wittman, B., Kofler, J., Beyer, J., Lita, A., Calkins, B., Gerrits, T., Nam, S. W., Ursin, R., Zeilinger, A. (2012, 3 December). Bell Violation With Entangled Photons, Free of the Fair-Sampling Assumption. Nature 497(7448), 227-230. Retrieved from Cornell University Library: http://arxiv.org/abs/1212.0533

Gröblacher, S., Paterek, T., Kaltenbaek, R., Brukner, C., Zukowski, M., Aspelmeyer, M., & Zeilinger, A. (2007). An Experimental Test of Non-Local Realism. Nature, 446(7138), 871-875.

Hare, R. M. (1952). The Language of Morals. Oxford: The Clarendon Press.

Harnad, S. (1990). The Symbol Grounding Problem. Physica D: Nonlinear Phenomena, 42(1-3), 335-346.

Hawking, S. (1998). A Brief History of Time. New York: Bantam Books.

Hoefer, C. (2010, Spring). Causal Determinism. In Zalta, E. N. (Ed.), The Stanford Encyclopedia of Philosophy. Retrieved from HYPERLINK "https://plato.stanford.edu/archives/spr2010/entries/determinism-causal/" https://plato.stanford.edu/archives/spr2010/entries/determinism-causal/

Horgan, T. (2002). From Supervenience to Superdupervenience. In D. Chalmers (Ed.), Philosophy of Mind, Classical and Contemporary Readings (pp. 150-162). New York: Oxford University Press.

Hume, D. (1907). An Enquiry Concerning Human Understanding and Selections From A Treatise of Human Nature: With Hume's Authobiography and a Letter from Adam Smith (No. 45). Chicago: The Open Court Publishing Co.

Humphrey, N. (1999). A History of the Mind, Evolution and the Birth of Consciousness. New York: Copernicus Springer-Verlag.

Jackson, F. (2002). Epiphenomenal Qualia. In D. Chalmers (Ed.), Philosophy of Mind, Classical and Contemporary Readings (pp. 273-280). New York: Oxford University Press.

Jacob, P. (2010). Intentionality. In Zalta, E. N. (Ed.), The Stanford Encyclopedia of Philosophy. Retrieved from: http://plato.stanford.edu/entries/intentionality/

Jammer, M. (1973). Indeterminacy in Physics. In Dictionary of the History of Ideas, Vol 2 (pp. 586-594). New York: Charles Scribner & Sons.

Jammer, M. (1974). Philosophy of Quantum Mechanics: The Interpretations of Quantum Mechanics in Historical Perspective. USA: John Wiley and Sons.

Kane, R. (1996). The Significance of Free Will. New York: Oxford University Press.

Kim, J. (1982). Psychological Supervenience. Philosophical Studies, 41(1), 51-70.

Kim, J. (1993). Supervenience and Mind: Selected Philosophical Essays. London: Cambridge University Press.

Kim, J. (1998). Mind in a Physical World: An Essay on the Mind-Body Problem and Mental Causation. Cambridge, MA: MIT Press.

Kim, J. (2002). The Many Problems of Mental Causation. In D. Chalmers (Ed.), Philosophy of Mind, Classical and Contemporary Readings (pp. 170-179). New York: Oxford University Press.

REFERENCES

Ladyman, J., Ross, D., Spurrett, D., & Collier, J. (2010). Every Thing Must Go: Metaphysics Naturalized. New York: Oxford University Press.

Langton, R., & Lewis, D. (1988). Defining 'Intrinsic'. Philosophy and Phenomenological Research, 58(2), 333-345.

Leggett, A. J. (2003). Nonlocal Hidden-Variable Theories and Quantum Mechanics: An Incompatibility Theorem. Foundations of Physics, 33(10), 1469-1493.

Lewis, D. (2007). On the Plurality of Worlds. In H. Beebee, & J. Dodd (Eds.), Reading Metaphysics: Selected Texts with Interactive Commentary (pp. 209-212). Maiden, MA: Blackwell Publishing.

Lloyd, S. (2000). Ultimate Physical Limits to Computation. Nature, 406(6799), 1047-1054.

Loureiro, A., Cuceu, A., Abdalla, F. B., Moraes, B., Whiteway, L., McLeod, M., Balan, S. T., Lahav, O., Benoit-Levy, A., Manera, M., Rollins, R. P., & Xavier, H. S. (2019). Upper Bound of Neutrino Masses from Combined Cosmological Observations and Particle Physics Experiments. Physical Review Letters 123(8), 081301.

Loux, M. J. (2006). Metaphysics, a Contemporary Introduction (Third Edition). New York: Routledge.

Maloof, J. N., Whangbo, J., Harris, H. M., Jongeward, G. D., & Kenyon, C. (1999). A Wnt Signaling Pathway Controls Hox Gene Expression and Neuroblast Migration in C. elegans. Development 126(1), 37-49.

McDaniel, K. (2010). John M. E. McTaggart. In Zalta, E. N. (Ed.), The Stanford Encyclopedia of Philosophy. Retrieved 2010 from: http://plato.stanford.edu/entries/mctaggart/

McTaggart, J. (1927). The Nature of Existence (2 volumes). Cambridge: Cambridge University Press.

Metcalfe, H. C., Williams, J. E., & Castka, J. F. (1980). Modern Chemistry. New York: Holt, Rinehart & Winston.

Nagel, T. (2002). What Is It Like to Be a Bat? In D. Chalmers (Ed.), Philosophy of Mind, Classical and Contemporary Readings (pp. 219-226). New York: Oxford University Press.

Oaklander, N. (1994). A Defense of the New Tenseless Theory of Time. In N. Oaklander, & Q. Smith (Eds.), The New Theory of Time (pp. 57-68). New Haven: Yale University Press.

O'Connor, T. (2009). Free Will. The Stanford Encyclopedia of Philosophy. Retrieved from: HYPERLINK "https://plato.stanford.edu/entries/freewill/" https://plato.stanford.edu/entries/freewill/

Oshio, K., Iwasaki, Y., Morita, S., Osana, Y., Gomi, S., Akiyama, E., Kawamura, K. (2003). Database of Synaptic Connectivity of C. elegans for Computation: Technical Report of CCeP, Keio Future, No. 3, Keio University. Retrieved 2010 from: http://ims.dse.ibaraki.ac.jp/ccep/

Page, D. N., & Wootters, W. K. (1983). Evolution without Evolution: Dynamics Described by Stationary Observables. Physical Review D (Particles and Fields), 27(12), 2885-2892.

Parisi, G., & Sourlas, N. (1979). Random Magnetic Fields, Supersymmetry, and Negative Dimensions. Physical Review Letters, 43(11), 744-745.

Place, U. T. (2002). Is Consciousness a Brain Process? In D. Chalmers (Ed.), Philosophy of Mind, Classical and Contemporary Readings (pp. 55-60). New York: Oxford University Press.

Plato, White, N. P. (Tr.) (1997). The Sophist. In Cooper, J. M. (Ed.), Plato, Complete Works (pp. 247d-e). Indianapolis: Hackett Publishing.

Potter, F. (2010). No Time for Quarks! FQXi Essay Contest: 2008 The Nature of Time Winning Essays. Retrieved 2010 from: http://www.fqxi.org/community/essay/winners/2008.1

Putnam, H. (1973). The Nature of Mental States. In D. Chalmers (Ed.), Philosophy of Mind, Classical and Contemporary Readings (pp. 73-79). New York: Oxford University Press.

Quine, W. V. (1948). On What There Is. The Review of Metaphysics 2 (5), 21-38.

Quine, W. V. (1969). Ontological Relativity & Other Essays. New York: Columbia University Press.

Reichenbach, H. (1958). The Philosophy of Space & Time. Mineola, New York: Dover Publications, Inc.

Reid, T. (1969). Essays on the Intellectual Powers of Man. Essay 2. Cambridge, MA: MIT Press.

Rosenfeld, W., Burchardt, D., Garthoff, R., Redeker, K., Ortegel, N., Rau, M., & Weinfurter, H. (2017). Event-Ready Bell Test Using Entangled Atoms Simultaneously Closing Detection and Locality Loopholes. Physical Review Letters, 119(1), 010402.

Rosenfeld, W., Weber, M., Volz, J., Henkel, F., Krug, M., Cabello, A., Zukowski, M., & Weinfurter, H. (2009). Towards a Loop-Free Test of Bell'sInequality With Entangled Pairs of Neutral Atoms. Advanced Science Letters, 2(4), 469-474. Retrieved from Cornell University Library: http://arxiv.org/abs/0906.0703v1

Rovelli, C. (1996). Relational Quantum Mechanics. International Journal of Theoretical Physics, 35(8), 1637–1678.

Rovelli, C. (2008). Forget Time. FQXi Essay Contest: 2008 The Nature of Time Winning Essays. Retrieved 2010 from: http://www.fqxi.org/community/essay/winners/2008.1

Rovelli, C., & Smolin, L. (1995). Spin Networks and Quantum Gravity. Physical Review D, 52(10), 5743-5759.

Russell, B. (1919). Mysticism and Logic. New York: Longmans, Green and Co.

Searle, J. R. (1980). Minds, Brains and Programs. Behavioral and Brain Science, 3, 417-424.

Smolin, L. (2001). Three Roads to Quantum Gravity. New York: Basic Books.

Stein, G. (1993). Everybody's Autobiography. Cambridge, MA: Exact Change.

Stich, S. P. (1985). From Folk Psychology to Cognitive Science: The Case Against Belief. Cambridge, MA: MIT Press.

Taylor, E. F., & Wheeler, J. A. (1992). Spacetime Physics: Introduction to Special Relativity. New York: W. H. Freeman and Company.

van Fraassen, B. C. (1980). The Scientific Image. New York: Oxford University Press.

Vincente, A. (2006). On the Causal Completeness of Physics. International Studies in the Philosophy of Science, 20 (2), 149-171.

Watts, D., & Strogatz, S. (1998). Collective Dynamics of 'Small-World' Networks. Nature, 393(6684), 440-442.

Wheeler, J. A., & Ford, K. W. (1998). Geons, Black Holes, and Quantum Foam: A Life in Physics. New York: W. W. Norton & Company, Inc.

Wikimedia Commons. (2010). File: World line.svg. Retrieved from: http://en.wikipedia.org/wiki/File:World_line.svg

Woleński, J. (2010). Reism. In Zalta E. N. (ed.), The Stanford Encyclopedia of Philosophy: http://plato.stanford.edu/entries/reism/

Wolpert, D. H. (2008). Physical Limits of Inference. Physica D: Nonlinear Phenomena, 237(9), 1257-1281. Retrieved from www.arxiv.org/abs/0708.1362

Zimmerman, D. (2008). The Privileged Present: Defending an 'A-Theory' of Time. In T. Sider, J. Hawthorne, & D. Zimmerman (Eds.), Contemporary Debates in Metaphysics (pp. 211-225). Malden, MA: Blackwell.

REFERENCES

ENDNOTES— Time from Inside and Out—
a Scientifically Consistent View

[1] Current theories suggest that the universe consists of as many as ten or eleven dimensions, including the four dimensions of space and time. These theories all favor a universe where the dimensions exist within a physically closed universe, one in which physical laws are conserved and no outside forces are required for explanation.

[2] I shall not describe the intricate details of McTaggart's theory, with his claim to have found a proof of a contradiction. It rests on assumptions for properties to define both the A-series and the B-series. If the assumptions are accepted, it is generally conceded that the proof is logical. However, many philosophers reject at least some of the premises. I too find the basis in a property definition to fail.

[3] Admittedly the 4-tuple cartoon model is itself Newtonian and, therefore misleading, but it provides a jumping-off way to envision the following discussion and does not do violence to the argument.

[4] For many identical particles, the half-life is the time in which half the particles will decay. In a second half-life interval, half of the remaining particles will decay, and this pattern repeats. The lifetime of a particle is probabilistic, but overall probability laws govern.

[5] We are not in a neutral frame of reference per GR, due especially to Earth's gravity. Note that the clocks in orbit are closer to any concept of "unaffected time" since the satellites are effectively in free fall (around Earth). Our time is "less correct" if one thinks of time unaffected by gravitational or velocity effects to be somehow favored (although of course, no frame of reference is favored per relativity).

[6] Experiments were first performed by Hafele and Keating in 1971. The experiments were verified again in 1976 and afterward. See Alley (1981). The Global Positioning System (GPS)

accuracy depends on incorporating corrections for relativistic time dilation. This represents essentially a continuous experiment carried out every day by users of GPS.

[7] The effect of relativity is that the satellite's clocks run a net 38 μs per day faster than our clocks on Earth's surface, from the GR effect of 45 μs per day speeding up, and the SR effect of 7 μs per day slowing the satellite's clocks down.

[8] With our scientific instrumentation, we can observe a rapidly moving particle living a long time if it is moving past us fast. The experiment has been done many times. Particles moving fast past us take longer to decay.

[9] Elsewhere I advance a radically different ontology, with causality not from particles. See the accompanying paper entitled, *A Metaphysical Ontology Consisting Only of Relations*.

[10] From Wikimedia Commons (2010).

[11] A cartoon particle model is used to simplify the explanation. No commitment to a particle model is implied, and the explanation only serves the purpose of exploring the endurantist argument.

[12] Ladyman et al. echo this point, saying that such foliation between space and time are only valid relative to a particular inertial frame and, therefore, "This seems to imply eternalism, since if there is no privileged foliation of space–time, then there is no global present, and so the claim that future events are not real does not refer to a unique set of events" (2010, p. 163).

[13] The Wheeler-DeWitt equation, developed in the 1960s, attempted to find compatibility between theories of quantum mechanics and general relativity, toward a theory of quantum gravity, to avoid infinities in the equations. However, the equation indicated the counterintuitive result that time played no role, leading to the 'problem of time.' This problem might be overcome as proposed by Page and Wootters (1983), based on quantum entanglement. Their result might suggest that time is an emergent phenomenon because of

the nature of entanglement. It would suggest that time exists only for observers within the universe.

[14] The perception described is a physical, not a psychological one. Our atomic clocks confirm that time is flowing, for example, by measuring the electron transition frequency of the electromagnetic spectrum of atoms. Such causality relationships, in this example between atoms, is evidence to explain the flow of time viewed from within the universe.

ENDNOTES— A Metaphysical Ontology Consisting Only of Relations

[1] Quine's seminal paper, *On What There Is*, is a guidepost to philosophers seeking a simple and elegant ontology. Quine suggests clearing out the profusion of entities from philosophical ontology, in favor of desert landscapes. (See Quine W. V., 1948.)

[2] I shall skip over the extensive literature regarding the problem of universals and nominalism.

[3] The phrase originates in Medieval philosophy, having some foundation in the thing (from the Latin, *fundamentum in re*).

[4] Philosophers have looked for truthmakers as the elements existing in reality that make the proposition true. Without truthmakers, a philosophical dilemma arises to explain any basis for truth. If such truthmakers exist, then the question arises as to the ontological characterization of truthmakers, and one response has been to consider truthmakers as properties. The brief introduction of truthmakers glosses over a rich philosophical discussion, including such distinctions as between truth-bearers and truthmakers, the focus of which is on truth-making between predicates in analytic sentences and whether truthmakers themselves are properties or are relations between other entities (such as between propositions or facts). See, for example, Clementz (2007) and Rovelli (2008).

⁵ More precisely, the four fundamental forces are modeled as fields. A field has a value for each point in space–time, and is considered to have physical reality. A set of mathematical rules characterize each field, specifying the relationship among the points. The description of fields fits neatly with the proposed ontology for relations.

⁶ van Fraassen says of scientific realism, "Science aims to give us, in its theories, a literally true story of what the world is like; and acceptance of a scientific theory involves the belief that it is true" (1980, p. 8). Ladyman et al. say, ". . . scientific realism is the view that we ought to believe that our best current scientific theories are approximately true, and that their central theoretical terms successfully refer to the unobservable entities they posit" (2010, p. 68).

⁷ Admittedly this seems to fit the "neo-Scholastic metaphysics" approach that Ladyman et al. rightly criticize (2010, p. 7, section 1.2), but I hope to allay that objection by the close of the argument through reliance on scientific results as the arbiter.

⁸ The restriction of a physically closed universe is a philosophical one, not an astrophysical one. The philosopher Kim articulated this tenet for a physicalist view as the principle that "if you pick any physical event and trace out its causal ancestry or posterity, that will never take you outside the physical domain" (2002, p. 175). In contrast, in physical cosmology, the term refers to the global geometry of the universe, with possible shapes including flat (zero curvature), open (negative curvature), and closed (positive curvature).

⁹ Note that this bare statement is provisional, only a starting point, because one must begin with *something* having existence. (I will later reverse this statement.) An object as defined has some correspondence to the Aristotelian category of *substance*, but I prefer the term *object* to suggest a discrete or quantized universe, and to highlight the issues surrounding dimensionality and philosophical questions of

how we might think about properties inhering in substance or object.

[10] For geometers who may object that particles have existence, while points are strictly dimensionless (and arguably lack an essential characteristic of existence), my argument will address the issue.

[11] I am concerned with properties of or relations between objects that exist, and therefore I do not address nonexistence except in passing, recognizing only the logical implication for nonexistence. I do not consider existence (instantiation) as a relation. This avoids the problem of Bradley's regress, which would suggest an infinite regress of relations in order to relate any two objects. For Bradley's regress see Bradley (1893, p. 57).

[12] This is a simplistic portrayal for multiple reasons, and one is that, under GR, the space–time coordinate structure is dependent upon relations within it. For any collection of objects, when the property of mass (or energy) is exhibited, mass warps space and time. According to GR, relations among objects have effects from the smallest to the largest scales, and on the overall spatiotemporal structure of the universe. Note that virtual particles are constantly popping in and out of existence, and some have mass. For example, the LEP collider at CERN produced Z bosons and measured their mass, demonstrating that the Z spent some time as a virtual top quark. Mass warps such a spaciotemporal construct and therefore it is never stable, as the simplistic portrayal might suggest. The cartoon construct serves as a pictorial to aid in explanation.

[13] Let me emphasize again that, at this point in the argument, I've used a cartoon construct to aid in visualizing my major point. Moreover, this point about existence (now provisional) will ultimately be reversed in the argument. This cartoon construct ignores several concepts in physics (which, by the end of the argument, will be irrelevant to the point). Rather

than this cartoon construct, physics describes space–time as filled with fields. Vibrations in the fields are called particles. In QM, there is only the wave function with a corresponding probability distribution. The bare philosophical statement regarding existence admittedly contradicts quantum theory, wherein an object does not exist at a specific point until a measurement is made, when the wave function collapses. Alternatively, in Everett & Wheeler's "many worlds" interpretation, no collapse is necessary. Quantum theory concludes that the Schrödinger equation describes the quantum state of a physical system, and the theory is exceedingly well supported by experiment. That evidence and result is not challenged here. By the conclusion of the discourse, I suggest that causation operates in a hidden dimension, with the results obtained in space–time consistent with the Schrödinger equation. See Eisberg & Resnick (1985, pp. 124-167) for further description of Schrödinger's theory.

[14] Our common talk of existent objects is of macroscopic objects—rocks, trees, people. Such macroscopic objects then might be composed of a collection of smallest elements, whatever they might be, and existent at some (generally contiguous) collection of points in space–time. I add the caveat that this is a provisional starting point only to make the argument intelligible given our use of language derived from our viewpoint embedded in the universe. By the end I hope to demonstrate that I haven't fallen into the trap of extending the manifest image, one of a special manifold comprising material objects; see Ladyman, Ross, Spurrett, & Collier (2010, p. 21).

[15] In this context, existence monism refers to a philosophy holding that the universe is composed of only one concrete object. As one example, the philosopher Spinoza may have been advocating existence monism, with an eternal unity manifest in the substance of God.

[16] I add one caveat to this statement further on in my argument: relations are predicated on the existence *or nonexis-*

REFERENCES

tence of objects. It will be seen that my focus is not on the objects but instead on the relations among objects (whether such objects are existent or not). Objects take on the role of markers used to define the relations.

[17] For physicists impatient with the description, let me emphasize that this is a cartoon model merely to facilitate understanding, not a conjecture about how the physical universe operates. The cartoon model imagines that some real element, some object, either exists or does not exist at each coordinate. Such objects then might include fields. Vibrations in the fields are called particles.

[18] I suspect that mathematically one may describe these polyadic relations either as n-tuples, or as multiples of paired relations of the form (a,b).

[19] Macroscopic objects then are collections of (mostly) adjacent smallest objects, operating together in a pattern, determined by some causal rule or process. For example, the planet Neptune is a collection of molecules of rock, ices and gases, and those are composed of smaller components concluding with smallest objects. Geology, chemistry, and physics do fine work to describe this macroscopic object. We label the macroscopic object "Neptune" and a "planet" because those labels reflect how humans experience Neptune, observing that gravitationally bound collection of molecules.

[20] Quine offered the example of a "possible fat man in that doorway" (1969, p. 43) to criticize the proliferation of ontological entities by certain philosophers, some who proposed that 'possibles' have real existence. By the model presented here, we may explain why we may have discourse about such possibles without admitting any new entity into ontology.

[21] Admittedly, our finite observable universe may be a part of an infinite total universe, or even a multiverse. If you like your universes infinite, you are welcome to them. Rather than finding wonder in infinities that are hard to fully imagine, my approach here is to find wonder in a radically different way by envisioning what may be a single, finite universe.

[22] Since a quark is considered an elementary particle, it would not have internal structure. The quark wave packet occupies nonzero volume, and the resulting diameter is of this scale.

[23] Wheeler first proposed that space–time might exhibit "foamy," uneven character at the Planck scale. See Wheeler & Ford (1998).

[24] The principle says that uncertainties occur when simultaneously measuring momentum and position and the energy and time variables of a particle. See Eisberg & Resnick (1985, pp. 65-69).

[25] Locke coined the alternative terms primary and secondary qualities, which are synonymous with primary and secondary properties.

[26] However, at the scale of 10^{-15} m, a single electron or proton could be in motion.

[27] For example, the photon, gluon, and the predicted graviton have zero mass (Eisberg & Resnick, 1985, p. 35). (In contrast, at another size scale, a radio photon, with zero invariant mass, is many kilometers long.) The current Standard Model of quantum theory would characterize all particles as lacking mass without the Higgs mechanism, operating through the Higgs field and Higgs boson. But the Higgs boson operates in relation to other particles to account for mass. Certain elementary particles such as quarks can be better described in physical formulas as dimensionless point particles, because they have no internal structure and act as if all their matter were in one point. However, the Heisenberg uncertainty principle in quantum mechanics would suggest that even in these cases, the wave packet of the particle has a non-zero dimension, and that 4-D space–time is granular at its smallest scale. Therefore, current theory has not yet omitted "dimension" from the lexicon, though the physics approaches complete description in mathematical terms.

[28] Given our current physics, it is not possible to claim that all properties might be eliminated in favor of relations. But there are hints that more of the properties associated with

the subatomic world may be expressed in relations. Many of the partial theories of quantum gravity, such as twistor theory and loop quantum gravity, suggest a focus on the relations among elements, and do not assume that properties play a role in the form resembling a property found in philosophy.

[29] The hypothesis centers on the possible causative powers of relations. It looks back to Plato's Eleatic stranger, in search of *what is*, those elements which have *capacity*. It is most interested in what makes the watch go. With regard to causation, this argument goes opposite to Russell's eliminativism (1919, p. 180). Here it is asserted that philosophers have a proper role to pose metaphysical hypotheses that may be tested by science. Left to its own, science tends to "shut up and calculate." Then it may face the situation of the drunk, having lost his keys, who searches under a lamppost because the light is better. Physics continues to search under the particle lamppost. I argue for scientists and metaphysicians to search together for the "cement of the universe." Ladyman et al. say, "The causation as glue tradition contains a substantial body of work, developing what are collectively called causal process theories. Such glue would be or would provide the necessity that Hume couldn't find in the impressions and their regular relations. Causal process theories, that is, can be understood as attempts to answer Hume's epistemological challenge to say how anyone could know, by any amount of observation, which links between processes are causal and which are not" (2010, p. 262).

[30] Forces and fields, of which many have theoretically infinite ranges, are particularly well accounted for by PCRs within this metaphysical framework.

[31] Certain current partial theories of quantum gravity suggest the focus on the relations between processes. For example, Penrose's twistor theory postulates causal processes as the main elements, and these are composed of events in space–time. See Smolin (2002, Ch. 4).

[32] Philosophers have looked for truthmakers for particular truths as the elements existing in reality that make the proposition true. Without truthmakers, a philosophical dilemma arises to explain any basis for truth. If such truthmakers exist, then the question arises as to the ontological characterization of truthmakers, and one response has been to consider truthmakers as properties. The brief introduction of truthmakers glosses over a rich philosophical discussion, including such distinctions as between truth-bearers and truthmakers, the focus of which is on truth-making between predicates in analytic sentences, and whether truthmakers themselves are properties or are relations between other entities (such as between propositions or facts). See, for example, Clementz (2007) and Rovelli (2008).

[33] Relying on the fundamental distinction between PCRs and NCRs, I do not follow the classification of truthmakers proposed by other philosophers. In my approach PCRs embody a certain truth-making in nature, and some NCRs embody truth-making for information.

[34] To be precise, two examples need elaboration "all the way down." Let me return to the example of a relation between a molecule of ammonia on Jupiter and the period at the end of this sentence. There are two PCRs: a pattern of relations constituting a molecule of ammonia, and the period, a pattern of relations constituting the graphite smudge. The relation between these two collections of PCRs is an NCR. That NCR only has meaning as a counterexample. However, a counterexample is meaningful in mathematical logic, and therefore this NCR has nominal value as a truthmaker. In similar fashion, Fodor's unintended counterexample is an NCR, though not a PCR.

[35] Physicists might find the resulting ontological framework will lead to better models of reality that have testable predictions. The test of the hypothesis can only be made by science looking to the natural world.

REFERENCES

[36] I say "rational" in the Rational tradition in philosophy, though the overall argument is empirical, relying on the evidence from physics suggesting that traditional ontology cannot be correct.

[37] A gymnast executes a handstand starting with hands straight overhead, then lunges forward to place both hands on the floor. The resulting position is upside down and facing backward from the starting position. This metaphysical hypothesis also lunges in a radical new direction, and then ends with the observer reoriented in two dimensions.

[38] Abstract algebras seem to explain, at least partially so far, certain fundamental aspects of the universe as found in theories in mathematical physics. Abstract algebras work with ordered pairs (a,b) in groups, rings, and other abstract structures. Ordered pairs may correspond to the points or objects designating the ends of causative relations.

[39] We have lived with a scientific conception of atoms for only about a century. In the seventeenth century, Newton imagined "corpuscles" to describe light. But the natural philosophers were not completely convinced. In the eighteenth century, Young's experiments seemed to prove the wave nature of light, and this view persisted until early twentieth-century experiments. Rutherford's classic experiments seemed to reveal hidden atomic structure, when alpha particles were deflected off points (something?) within the nucleus of atoms of gold foil. Bohr's description of the atom as a nucleus surrounded by orbiting electrons captured the imagination, and this solar-system model has been an earworm even after quantum physics denied such a physical structure. The current model of the atom is sometimes described with a cloud of electrons surrounding the nucleus, with electrons existing as a smeared quantum wave. Physicists use their instruments to probe this posited entity of the atom, assumed by many to have real existence in a real location in space–time, with our ability to know their metrics governed by the Heisenberg uncertainty principle.

[40] I say nonhierarchical because there is no metaphysical reason to imagine "levels" in the ontology, as some philosophers wish to require levels in nature. There need only be PCRs arranged in patterns. The greater causative power that we may attribute to, say, macroscopic objects, would be due just to larger patterns of the same constitutive elements.

[41] The existence of booms might provide an ontological basis for number.

[42] This is reminiscent of "turtles all the way down," the trope variously employed by John Locke, David Hume, William James, Bertrand Russell, and Stephen Hawking, among others (Hawking, 1998).

[43] See the accompanying paper entitled, *Time from Inside and Out—a Scientifically Consistent View*.

[44] The universe is "empty" relative to the density of objects that we experience, but current theory suggests it is filled with both dark energy and dark matter particles. The density of both are low, with dark energy and dark matter throughout the universe each estimated at a density less than 10^{-29} g/cm^3.

[45] The visible universe is on the order of 10^{27} m if one includes an expansion factor of ~3.2 from current expansionary theories of the universe.

[46] The hard vacuum has densities of hydrogen estimated as low as an atom per cubic meter.

[47] Our notion of passing time is intertwined in the result. GR suggests that space–time is one continuum. Therefore, bolts might form patterns across the entire continuum.

[48] The paper authored by Einstein, Podolsky, and Rosen espoused the view described as "local realism," suggesting that quantum theory could not be a complete theory, but must be supplemented by other variables to account for locality and causality. See Einstein, Poldolsky, & Rosen (1935).

[49] The hidden variables in question are hidden because they are not part of quantum theory, not because they are locally

hidden. However, for the experiments performed by Aspect and others, the results amount to the same conclusion.

[50] As examples of work to remove loopholes from tests of Bell's inequalities, see Clauser & Horne (1974), Rosenfeld, et al. (2009), and Giustina, Mech, Ramelow, Wittman, & Kofler (2012). Recent work has closed the detection and locality loopholes simultaneously (Rosenfeld, et al., 6 July 2017).

[51] The description assumes that the principle of counterfactual definiteness holds, which is not true in all interpretations of quantum theory. If counterfactual definiteness holds, then the principle of locality must be violated if Bell's inequalities are violated.

[52] Others have offered relational alternatives for the violation of Bell's inequalities, including Filk. (Filk, 2006).

[53] See the accompanying paper entitled, *Mental Causation—a Relational Ontology*.

[54] Ibid.

[55] Many contemporary philosophers accept a deterministic description of the universe, where free will is difficult to entertain. Incompatibalists argue that free will and determinism are incompatible. Other philosophers, compatibilists, have attempted to carve out some form of free will within a deterministic universe. For example, Dennett (2007) offered a limited form of free will within a deterministic universe by abandoning the "could have done otherwise" stipulation. In contrast, the discussion here looks to a robust definition of free will—one worth having.

[56] Kane notes, "Critics argue that undetermined events in the brain or body would occur spontaneously and would be more of a nuisance—or perhaps a curse, like epilepsy—than an enhancement of the agent's freedom" (1996, p. 10).

[57] An earlier similar example was offered by Compton (1931), using as apparatus a double slit with a photon passing through a slit to determine whether a stick of dynamite will be exploded.

ENDNOTES— Mental Causation—a Relational Ontology

[1] See the accompanying paper entitled, *A Metaphysical Ontology Consisting Only of Relations*.

[2] At base in emergentist philosophical theories, there generally is either an explicit or implicit reliance on the ontological emergence of mentality. My relational ontology finds such ontological emergence unnecessary. Panpsychism holds that all matter has a mental aspect. The relational ontology denies this ontological claim.

[3] Hypotheses in philosophy of mind about the nature of mentality, and examples and analogies to illustrate them, can have a detrimental effect if small analogical inconsistencies are overlooked in an effort toward theory consistency. The examples and analogies may thereby disguise the real ontology of mind. For these reasons, a biological exemplar will serve to direct the philosophical argument and to keep it rooted in the physical reality of biological sciences. For a physicalist, any ontology of mind must be consistent with empirical results, and with the biological world that we find around us.

[4] I will focus on the presentation of Kim's argument reprinted in Chalmers (2002), acknowledging that it is an excerpt of a longer work (Kim, 1998).

[5] Not all philosophers agree with Kim's definition. For example, Ladyman et al. opt for a definition directly from scientists, saying, "Physicalism is generally regarded, at least by most physicalists, as a naturalist position that is motivated by science" (2010, p. 39).

[6] Note, on the contrary, that the relational ontology leads to reductionist interpretations of mentality.

[7] I will have more to say to parse Kim's distinction between "extrinsic mental properties" and "relational properties" in Section 3, but here focus on Kim's assessment of syntacticalism.

REFERENCES

[8] Kotarbiński's table of ontological categories propose two theses: (a) any object is a thing, and (b) no object is a state of affairs, relation, or property. See Woleński (2010, pp. 4-8).

[9] Regarding properties, however, I will differ fundamentally with Quine, as he always accepted the existence of properties as essential to predication.

[10] To explicitly place this ontology within the philosophical conversation, I claim a reductive physicalist ontology for the mind. Chalmers' definitions for these terms are sufficient when referring to the mind generally and by extension to consciousness. Chalmers says, "A *reductive explanation* of consciousness will explain this wholly on the basis of physical principles that do not themselves make any appeal to consciousness. A *materialist* (or physicalist) solution will be a solution on which consciousness is itself seen as a physical process" (p. 248). Using Chalmers' metaphysical classification of mind, I deny that the relational ontology is 'Type-F Monism' because I need not employ dualism, panpsychism, or mental properties that are a separate ontological kind. The suggested mental relations are non-hierarchical.

[11] The exemplar employed is a model animal versus a model plant. It is far easier to imagine how the interactions, on a time scale reasonably like our own, might allow the feedback loop with the environment to shape a primitive mentality that differs from mere digestion. I do not rule out, however, that such intentionality may develop in plants. Plants interact with their environments too. For example, when bark beetles attack California conifers, the trees react by producing defensive resinous pitch. But the slow environmental interactivity makes the argument challenging.

[12] The percentage of similar DNA between two organisms does not, of course, correlate with mental capacities. I argue that degree of mentality is driven by evolutionary adaptation pressures and the demands of particular ecologies. This DNA similarity shows that *C. elegans* and *Homo sapiens* are undoubtedly part of the same biological continuum.

[13] The biological sciences are demonstrating the direct connections between *C. elegans* and *Homo sapiens*. For example, the Hox genes are a group of genes that appear in humans and in other living creatures. They encode homeodomain proteins that specify the anterior-posterior axis and segment identity of organisms during embryonic development. Certain Hox genes have also been found in *C. elegans*, such as the Hox gene mab-5 (Maloof, Whangbo, Harris, Jongeward, & Kenyon, 1999).

[14] Admittedly, *memories and beliefs* may be further described as stored, prior mental events, so the definition of mental events is recursive, but in a fashion that I think can be supported by an empirical, evolutionary explanation.

[15] I use the terms *lower map* and *upper map* with no other connotation than to linguistically distinguish them.

[16] My guess is that the rate of underlying biochemical reactions dictates the particular temporality for life on Earth, and the dynamics of environmental ecology set a minimum speed constraint for maintenance of semantic meaning.

[17] Bermúdez notes that explanations of behavior traditionally have been either behavior-mechanistic or intentional explanations. He says that "Mechanistic explanations of behavior are appropriate when, and only when, the behavior to be explained can be specified in terms of non-relational bodily movements" (2003, p. 195), which is not the case in the examples given of *C. elegans*. Therefore *C. elegans* exhibits intentional behavior per Bermudez's distinction.

[18] Like many philosophical subjects, Brentano's claim, and the question of whether intentionality demonstrates either a necessary or sufficient condition for mentality is subject to various views. Many of the arguments describe both the nature of mentality and intentionality simultaneously, "proving what is not self-evident by means of itself" (Aristotle, 1984, p. 104). See Jacob (2010).

[19] Some may object that the following examples anthropomorphize *C. elegans*. I do not claim that I know what is really

going on inside the sparse mentality claimed for the creature, nor can any of us know what is like to be it, just as we cannot know what it is like to be a bat. The examples for needing food, moving to food, and eating food though do parallel our own mentality, and we would claim intentionality in carrying these activities out.

[20] The invented, simple notation takes the following form: Various mental states of the organism, such as perceptions and actions, are shown with capital letters (e.g., "N"). Collections of mental states are shown by conjoining individual mental states with the symbol "&." I use the symbol "→" to represent "results in," followed by the resulting mental state or combination of mental states. For example, "{N&~F→G}" symbolizes the internal sensing state "N," "need food," together with the external perceptual state "~F," "food not sensed," that result in the general locomotion action "G," "move around." Therefore, the notation "{N&~F→G}" refers to the relation of a mental event.

[21] Self-organization is found in generally open systems in which the internal organization increases in complexity without outside guidance. Many examples exist within physics and chemistry. Self-organization should not be conflated with emergence because self-organized examples exist without emergence. As one illustrative example, spontaneous folding of proteins is observed at the biochemical level in biology.

[22] I acknowledge Nicholas Humphrey (1999) for his ideas regarding external perception and internal sensation, which informed some of the hypothetical discussion here.

[23] The issues of syntax adequacy have been notably discussed by Searle and Block. A few comments on their arguments are in order. Searle's "Chinese Room" analogy (Searle, 1980), in which he argues that syntax is insufficient for semantics, also attacks computationalist approaches in which the brain processes a set of rules for manipulating symbols. In the analogy, Searle is locked in a room with boxes full of

Chinese symbols, and a rule book that enables him to answer questions put to him in Chinese (of which he has no understanding). Searle can process the symbols to pass the Turing test for understanding Chinese. Yet since he does not understand Chinese, Searle argues that neither does any other computer program. Searle's analogy cleverly demonstrates that the Chinese Room does not instantiate semantics; therefore, syntax is insufficient for mentality.

The relational mental ontology suggests that no semantics is instantiated in the Chinese Room because no fully formed mental relation exists. By this view, Searle does not understand Chinese; the system of the Chinese Room does not understand Chinese; neither Searle nor the system of the Chinese Room instantiate a semantics. Like the following example of my cell phone with a button that together lack any semantics (without my presence to provide meaning to the button), the Chinese Room requires an outside observer who understands Chinese symbols to provide any semantics. The critical point is not that Searle lacks an understanding of Chinese, but rather that semantics is created through an ongoing relational instantiation. (If Searle understood Chinese, then Searle *simpliciter* would understand Chinese, and the Chinese Room system would be extraneous to semantics.) Mentality exists only when the semantics is intrinsic to, and arises as a result of, the instantiation of the relation. The broad span of the relation is required—linking in a single mental event the external environment and the organism's internal states—to create meaning. The relational mental ontology eliminates *exclusive* dependence on symbols or representations "in the machine."

An important distinction is made here from the 'systems reply.' The systems reply to Searle asserts that the entire system understands Chinese though Searle does not. Following the computer analogy, the systems reply says that Searle is performing the role of the CPU within the system. In contrast to the systems reply, the relational ontology asserts that the system of the Chinese Room lacks the necessary conditions to instantiate a semantics.

Since this explication is in the business of addressing analogies in philosophy of mind, I should note Ned Block's "Chinese Nation" analogy (Block, 2002), in which he imagines the billion people of China connected by radio transmitters, implementing the functions of neurons in a brain. Block's "Chinese Nation" exhibits the same problem as Searle's Chinese Room. According to the relational mental ontology, since the Chinese Nation does not maintain an ongoing semantics embracing the dynamically changing environment, no mental activity is instantiated.

[24] This description conjures up Chalmers' analogy of the conscious thermometer. I deny that a simple flow of biochemicals, or operation of a thermometer, is in any form conscious. First, the examples from *C. elegans* do not describe consciousness. Second, the mental ontology requires three relations and the appearance of a primitive semantics that is more than mechanistic. But it does raise the question of when a set of mechanistic biochemical processes are complex enough to constitute nonconscious sparse mentality. An evolutionary argument necessarily begins without mentality or intentionality and must present a reasonable path to both without a gap. I suggest whenever (a) sets of relations of mental events span from internal states to states in the environment, and (b) the sets of relations exhaust a logical span of responses, then the conditions are trivially met. The case described is of such a paired set of either (a) sensing nutrients and consuming nutrients, or (b) sensing no nutrients and then moving until nutrients are sensed. This conceivably might be the first trivial example of a sufficient relationship to constitute sparse mentality in biology on Earth. Turning to *C. elegans*, since it observationally has a suite of logical responses (for feeding, movement, avoidance of det-

rimental environmental conditions, and reproduction), my claim is that *C. elegans* exhibits the intentionality sufficient for nonconscious sparse mentality.

[25] Referring to the ancient algorithm for finding all prime numbers up to any given limit. In like manner, it is asserted that evolution has sorted through the true semantic connections—the ones that perform the task of keeping the organism alive and competitive in its ecological landscape.

[26] Evolution had plenty of opportunities to sort useful reactions from useless reactions. A few figures hint at the scales involved. First, there likely was of the order of 100-200 million years between the time that Earth became conducive to life and the actual onset of life. A typical bacterium (such as *E. coli*) divides in about 20 minutes; therefore, if unlimited nutrient supplies are available, 2^{72} bacteria might exist after a single day. Given the exponential character of the mathematics, theoretically the mass of biological material (if unrestricted) rapidly exceeds the mass of Earth. Of course, the current discussion is about biochemical reactions. For elementary conversions of metabolites, the rough reaction times are of the order of 10 milliseconds per reaction. Therefore, the number of variations explored would be many orders of magnitude <u>more</u> than given by the example of dividing bacteria.

[27] Kim argues against syntactic theories such as those of Stephen Stich (1985).

[28] The relational mental ontology prompts speculations regarding how an evolutionary path from primitive relations might progress to richly inscribed mentality that includes memory. As one example, perhaps the so-called mirror neurons might have evolved from a normal muscle-neuron firing relational endpoint, into energy-conserving new roles for kinesthetic memory.

[29] For the relational mental ontology to hold, it suggests that every biological life form must "boot up" with inaugurating relational instantiations, starting with first sensory impres-

sions. From these rudimentary beginnings, the inherited neural machinery replaces portions of the relations with more efficient addendums (instantiating memories). The more sophisticated the organism, the more intricate these mechanisms would be, all developed through evolutionary selection. There is a role for complex early development stages in the life cycle, which would be encouraged by evolution, to make mentality more robust.

[30] I've limited further discussion of natural kinds and believe that replacing it with *relations* clarifies the ontology of mental activity. I wish to resist expanding my ontology beyond physical objects and the relations among physical objects, eschewing the metaphysical discussion regarding the ontological status of natural kinds. Related to this debate is the semantic discussion of to what natural kinds refer. For an example of theories of reference, Kripke said that a natural kind gives a necessary identity across possible worlds. Note that many philosophers embrace a richer description of natural kinds than used here. My approach more closely follows Quine in his paper *Natural Kinds* (1969, p. 134). Noting how scientific advancement redefines kinds, he says "man continues his rise from savagery, sloughing off the muddy old notion of kind or similarity piecemeal, a vestige here and a vestige there."

[31] Note that semantics is created from the inside out, from the entity's point of view. We cannot determine whether our nematode can distinguish "anxiety" from "hunger;" this is dependent upon the granularity of semantic meaning in the particular organism.

[32] The empirical details do make a difference to the speed, scale and processing characteristics of the network. For example, the change from simple biochemical processes to neural processes would allow an enormous increase in speed and specificity of connection.

[33] See the accompanying paper entitled, *A Metaphysical Ontology Consisting Only of Relations*.

www.ingramcontent.com/pod-product-compliance
Lightning Source LLC
Chambersburg PA
CBHW031122080526
44587CB00011B/1078